Skateboarding
From Dogtown to the X-Games

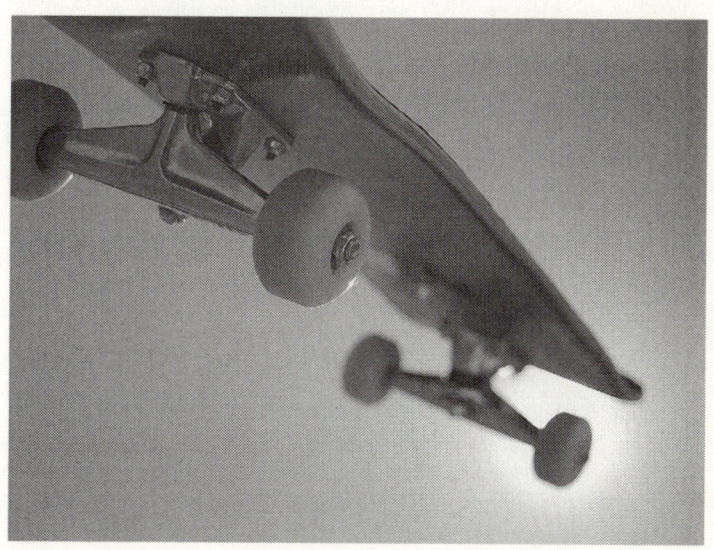

Tom Peacock

© 2006 by OverTime Books
First printed in 2006 10 9 8 7 6 5 4 3 2 1
Printed in Canada

All rights reserved. No part of this work covered by the copyrights hereon may be reproduced or used in any form or by any means—graphic, electronic or mechanical—without the prior written permission of the publisher, except for reviewers, who may quote brief passages. Any request for photocopying, recording, taping or storage on information retrieval systems of any part of this work shall be directed in writing to the publisher.

The Publisher: OverTime Books is an imprint of Éditions de la Montagne Verte

Library and Archives Canada Cataloguing in Publication

Peacock, Tom, 1976–
    Skateboarding / Tom Peacock.

Includes bibliographical references.
ISBN-13: 978-1-897277-00-3
ISBN-10: 1-897277-00-8

   1. Skateboarding—History. 2. Skateboarders—Biography. I. Title.

GV859.8.P42 2006   796.22'09   C2006-903273-4

Project Director: J. Alexander Poulton
Cover & Title Page Images: Jiang Xiaobin. Courtesy Getty Images, photograph by Stanley Chou.

PC:P5

Dedication

To all the "fans" of my skateboarding:
One more try, okay? Then we go. I promise…

Contents

Preface:
Sidewalk Surfing......................... 6

Chapter 1:
The Early Days.......................... 8

Chapter 2:
The 1970s: Skateboarding Strikes Back... 13

Chapter 3:
Dogtown Dayz.......................... 16

Chapter 4:
Unsung Heroes of the 1970s............ 29

Chapter 5:
Alan's Ollie............................ 33

Chapter 6:
Powell Meets Peralta................... 37

Chapter 7:
Vert Punks Rule!....................... 40

Chapter 8:
Enter the Bones Brigade................ 52

Chapter 9:
Rodney Mullen: Untouchable........... 71

Chapter 10:
Straight to Video...................... 80

Chapter 11:
Vert's Troubled Prince.................. 86

Chapter 12:
Gator: Fall from Grace................. 95

Chapter 13:
The Rise of Street................. 104

Chapter 14:
Industry OVERhaul................ 116

Chapter 15:
Skateboarding's New Breed........ 123

Chapter 16:
Sponsor Me....................... 133

Chapter 17:
**The X-Games: Skateboarding
Meets Popular Culture**............. 144

Chapter 18:
Global Skateboarding Madness..... 150

Chapter 19:
**Danny Way:
Skateboarding's Next Frontier**..... 155

Notes on Sources................. 164

Preface

Sidewalk Surfing

Picture this. It's a warm summer day in 1965. A young girl sporting a dated hairdo and a shapeless dress cruises across the parking lot of the Canadian Broadcasting Corporation (CBC) in Toronto on a skateboard. The girl, 18-year-old Gai Cochrane, is the president of the Ontario branch of the National Sidewalk Surfers of Canada. CBC reporter Lloyd Robertson watches as she breezes across the asphalt, looking about as cool as it gets.

"Hi Gai!" enthuses Lloyd. "I'll bet this is the first time you've ever been on a skurf board in a dress as lovely as that!"

"Yes, it is," says Gai, smiling coyly.

"What do your parent's think of you skurfing?"

"Oh, they don't mind, as long as I'm careful and don't go on the roads too much."

"Why have you formed an association?" Lloyd asks, steering the interview in a more serious direction.

"Well, we were told by the Toronto Police that if we were in an organization, and a whole bunch of us got together, they wouldn't tell us to leave and take our boards away," Gai says.

"Is this really dangerous?" Lloyd asks.

"No, it's about as dangerous as bicycle riding. If you can control your board then it's alright, but if you can't, then you can injure yourself badly."

"Well, I'm going to ask you how to control this board a little later on, but we'll get to that in time. I understand there were some 40 fractures in Ottawa a couple of weekends ago, so it is dangerous if you don't know how to control the board..."

"Yes, it is. You can break your arm or your leg or...you can really take a bad fall if you're going too fast."

"Do you think this will be obsolete in time, like the hula-hoop?"

"No, I think it'll keep goin'."

Later, Lloyd makes a fairly stiff attempt to ride the board, with Gai supporting him, before the show cuts back to the host, Sandi Fruman, in the CBC studio. "Lloyd with Gai Cochrane, president of the National Sidewalk Surfers of Canada, Ontario Branch," Fruman says. "By the way, if sales in Montreal, Ottawa and Toronto are any indication, the fad may be dying out."

Skateboarding dying out? Yeah, right...

Chapter One

The Early Days

In 1965, skateboarding was a new menace taking over the streets, but Sandi Fruman was right when she announced on the CBC that the new fad was suffering some early growing pains. Even though it was just beginning to enter the cultural mainstream, sidewalk surfing's popularity was already cresting. Thanks to a rash of injuries (40 fractures in Ottawa in one weekend!) and a growing backlash from municipal officials and police across North America, the brand-new sport of skateboarding was suffering through its first public relations crisis by November of that year.

No matter how many associations Gai and her skurfing buddies started up, skateboarding was beginning to look too dangerous to a lot of people in authority positions and like too much of a liability for companies and stores worried about their bottom lines. Soon, under pressure from police and municipal officials, stores just stopped stocking skateboards, and the new companies manufacturing them were left with huge stockpiles of boards they couldn't sell.

Lousy wheels and boards were part of the problem. Of course, at the time, there was no precedent. Before companies started manufacturing boards, people who wanted to try skateboarding would simply tear the wheels and axles off their roller skates and nail them to a piece of wood. The first commercial boards churned out in the early 1960s were a godsend for kids around the world, even though they were unstable, heavy and slow. The Makaha factory in Santa Monica, California, went from dealing with orders for 74 boards a day to 2000 a day in just two years.

The first boards were narrow and flat, and the sketchy trucks (the axles connecting the wheels to the board) and unforgiving hard clay composite wheels on some of the better boards (surfing-inspired shapes manufactured by Makaha and its rivals Gordon & Smith (G&S), Val Surf and, later, Hobie) were only slightly better than the steel wheels and axles people had ripped off their roller skates in years past.

By 1965, the first skateboard companies had sold over 50 million boards, and a new magazine called *The Quarterly Skateboarder* had hit the stands. Editor John Severson was optimistic about the future of the sport. While he acknowledged the roots of skateboarding in surfing, he saw it as a sport with much more room for the development of maneuvers and techniques.

"Sure, sidewalk surfing's what it is, but we predict a lot more for skateboarding. We predict a real future for the sport—a future that could go as far as the Olympics," he wrote. "It's a much more "measurable" sport than surfing and therefore lends itself more to competition."

The skateboarders of the time began to make names for themselves by developing new tricks and styles of riding. By 1963, they were jumping over high bars, slaloming around cones and demonstrating the first flatland tricks, like 360 handstands and nose wheelies. Companies were forming teams and holding contests—the sport was booming.

Torger Johnson from Santa Monica, California, appears at the top of many skaters' lists of the most influential skateboarders of all time. He was one of the pioneers of freestyle skateboarding in the 1960s. In 1965, at the tender age of 12, Torger ruled the International Skateboard Championships in Anaheim, California, with his innovative moves, including a "pirouette." He placed first in the Tricks division and second overall. He also placed fourth in the flatland slalom event.

Torger's friend Bruce Logan, was also leading the skateboarding charge, along with his brothers Brian and Brad. Bruce Logan started skating in 1958 after tearing his roller skates to pieces and nailing the wheels to a piece of wood, just like other kids from that time were doing. Bruce and his brothers skated together, pushing each other to improve, and a few years later, in 1964, Bruce joined the Makaha team, the first-ever sponsored skateboard team.

At the "Internationals" in Anaheim in 1965, 13-year-old Bruce showed up with some impressive moves, including headstands on his board. He won a slew of contests, mostly in freestyle, throughout skateboarding's first wave and kept right on skating through the late '60s and early '70s, honing his craft before surging back into the competitive scene.

Steven and Dave Hilton, the sons of hotel mogul Baron Hilton, were also avid skateboarders by the time their father got into the business of skateboarding. Baron Hilton's juice company, Vita-Pakt, went into partnership with famed surfboard builder Hobie Alter and began manufacturing Hobie Skateboards in 1964. They put together the Hobie Super Surfer team, and soon after, the team set off across the country in a rented bus to promote the sports of surfing and skateboarding. Dave and Steve Hilton were on the Hobie team. Dave was also the skateboarder who appeared on the cover of the first-ever issue of *The Quarterly Skateboarder*. In the photo, Hilton, blond and barefoot, is pictured leaping over a bar about three feet off the ground as his clay-wheeled Hobie skateboard passes underneath.

Dave and his brother Steve were a big influence during skateboarding's first wave.

Other skaters, too, were at the forefront of skateboarding's progression: Danny Bearer, who rode for Hobie; Brad "Squeak" Blank, who won the first-ever skateboard contest at Hermosa Beach in California in 1963; Joey Cabell, who's credited with being the inventor of slalom skateboarding; Phil Edwards, an avid surfer turned skater; and John Freis, who's credited with inventing the nose wheelie.

During the latter half of the 1960s, the bottom fell out of skateboarding. Just as suddenly as orders for new boards had rushed in, they dried up. It's easy to blame the marriage of unforgiving pavement and shoddy equipment for the campaign against skateboarding that resulted in its rapid decline in popularity, but there were other, deeper forces at play. As skateboarder and writer Jocko Weyland explains, "It was something else, something less qualifiable about skating, that made it alarming. Kids were cavorting around without respect for authority, going unsupervised while engaging in an activity that most adults had never done and couldn't relate to. The kids were getting out of control."

It would be a few decades, though, before "the new terror loose in the streets of the city," as Sandi Fruman called skateboarding during that CBC broadcast way back in 1965, established itself as a bona fide presence in our society.

Chapter Two

The 1970s: Skateboarding Strikes Back

Some skaters, like Bruce Logan, kept right on riding through the 1960s, but most quit, at least temporarily. Almost a decade passed before skateboarding surged once again into the mainstream.

Tony Alva is generally considered to be the godfather of skateboarding in the 1970s. In an article published in *Thrasher* magazine two decades later, he recalled when the second wave of skateboarding began. He was at a schoolyard, and some of the legends from the previous decade were riding the asphalt banks like they were concrete waves.

"One day, just out of the blue, we pulled up on our bikes with our newly made woodshop custom cues. To our surprise, there were the legends that we had heard so much about. If I remember correctly, Steve and Davey Hilton, Danny Bearer, John Freis, Torger Johnson and Chris Piccolo were the first pros that we encountered. They walked the nose with ease, did toe spins at the top of the banks, heelies, 360s and soul arches. We were all amazed to see someone else show us what could really be done. My mind exploded with energy and ideas. I knew that what I was seeing would influence my riding, but I also wanted to take it in a unique direction of my own."

The resurgence of skateboarding's popularity was largely thanks to better equipment that made it safer and more enjoyable to experiment and pull moves while riding inclined surfaces at speed, like the ones Tony described. There was a whole new world of possibilities for getting radical on a board.

By 1971, Makaha founder Larry Stevenson had invented and patented the kicktail, making it much easier to maneuver the board. Two years later, surfer Frank Nasworthy's urethane wheels hit the marketplace. The new wheels, together with a better board and trucks designed specifically for skateboarding, changed the sport completely. As the caption below a picture of a Gordon & Smith Fibreflex board in the Skull Skates online museum states, real progression in skateboarding was now inevitable.

"The Bennett pro trucks turned like a mutha and the Road Rider wheels, with IKS bearings, rolled really smooth. Skating banks and ditches became a reality, now that equipment was getting dialed in, and people were starting to feel the stoke of building ramps. Although lots of the early ramps were 45-degree wedges made to mimic ditches rather than a pool."

Lots of new companies began getting in on the game. Bruce Logan and his family started the Logan Earth Ski Skateboard Company, manufacturing some of the bestselling boards of the era. Many of the top riders in the 1970s rode for Logan Earth Ski, including Torger Johnson, Tony Alva and Bob Biniak.

Skaters took to new surfaces with ease, and the sport's leading figures were constantly upping the ante, carving higher and faster in the drainage ditches and schoolyard banks of California. Then, when a drought hit Southern California in 1975, pools everywhere were left empty, and skateboarding's elite began making their way over backyard fences to find out how much further they could push themselves. Skaters had experimented with riding in empty pools in the '60s, but with such low-quality boards it was no surprise the idea didn't take off. In the 1970s, with the new equipment, that all changed.

Skating wasn't going to the Olympics, as John Severson had so optimistically predicted. Nevertheless, it was sticking around, finding its feet once again and going in a new direction, right into your backyard and into the empty swimming pool.

Chapter Three

Dogtown Dayz

We were so far ahead of what was going on in that zone it was amazing. I never realized we were different before that contest; the way we skated was the only way we knew how.

—Stacy Peralta, Skateboarder Magazine, 1976

One group in particular emerged in the 1970s to define skateboarding—the Z-Boys. Led by Tony Alva and Jay Adams, the gang from Dogtown would take skateboarding in an entirely new direction, cementing forever its reputation as an outsider activity, a subculture linked inextricably to the youthful desire for individual expression and adrenaline-fueled excitement.

In 1975, on a warm spring day in Del-Mar, California, the Zephyr skateboard team exploded onto the skateboarding scene during an event that would go down in the history books as a defining moment for skateboarding.

A board company out of Encinitas, California, Bahne skateboards had decided to stage the first major skateboard contest since the 1960s—the Bahne-Cadillac Del Mar Nationals. The format would be the same as the older contests, featuring slalom and freestyle events.

In the years since the skateboarding heydays of the early '60s, skateboarding had been developing in small, isolated pockets. One of them was the banked schoolyards of Los Angeles, California, where locals like Tony Alva and Stacy Peralta had begun taking surf-inspired moves to the pavement—not the traditional, more upright moves borrowed from surfing during the 1960s, but the smooth-flowing, low-riding, quick-turning moves of surfing's new breed, led by Hawaiian surfer Larry Bertleman. The group of young skaters idolized Bertleman and tried to emulate his low-riding style on the beach breaks of Santa Monica. They spent their time off the water riding their skateboards down Bicknell Hill, one block from their main hangout, the Zephyr surf shop. On their skateboards, as on their surfboards, they swooped as low as they could, their hands grazing the concrete as they slalomed through cones down the steep hill. Once they discovered the concrete waves surrounding the nearby schoolyards, skateboarding began to turn from being a way to pass the time when the water was flat to a full-on passion.

Soon Tony, Jay Adams, Stacy, Bob Biniak and the rest of what would eventually become the Zephyr skate team were spending hours and hours every day swooping up and down the schoolyard banks and, unbeknownst to them, leading the sport in a radical new direction.

Peggy Oki was the only girl on the Zephyr skateboard team. She started skating in the late '60s on clay wheels. Her brother made her a board in woodshop and kitted it out with the new urethane Cadillac wheels. Before long, Peggy was winding through cones on her way down Bicknell Hill and tearing across the asphalt banks at the nearby schoolyards with the other Z-Boys—Bob "The Bullet" Biniak, Wentzle Ruml, Jim Muir, Paul Constantineau and Shogo Kubo.

Shogo, who was born in Japan and moved to California as a teenager, was welcomed onto the team thanks to a hard-charging style that almost no one could match.

In 1975, Jeff Ho, Skip Engblom and Craig Stecyk, the three owners of the Zephyr surf shop, had begun producing skateboards. By the time the contest rolled around, they had a team, a T-shirt and enough attitude to ignite a revolution. They showed up at Del Mar with their ragtag team of skaters in tow ready to do just that.

Skateboarding's heroes of the day headed out onto the large, slick plywood surface set up at the

Bahne-Cadillac Nationals for the freestyle event. It had been so long since the last contest. What sort of moves were people going to bring to the floor? The old-school heroes were ready to handstand and nose wheelie their way to victory; they had no idea they were about to be upstaged by a small ragtag group of kids from the beach slums of Santa Monica.

The Zephyr team members showed up at the contest wearing their navy blue team T-shirts, jeans and matching Vans deck shoes, hair long and unkempt and shoes and jeans torn up from heavy sessions skating the schoolyard banks and sloloming through cones on the hills of Santa Monica, practicing for their world debut. Engblom, the self-appointed team manager, was wearing a zany, long-sleeved purple Hawaiian print shirt, a fedora, white dress shoes and dark sunglasses. The Zephyr team didn't fit in with the rest of the clean-cut crowd at the contest, and they knew it. But appearance was only a small part of it—the real shock would come when they finally got the chance to show what they could do on their skateboards.

The Zephyr juggernaut began when a skinny, blond-haired kid named Jay Adams entered the freestyle arena and proceeded to lay waste to everything skating had stood for. He tore around the raised platform, heading straight toward what looked like an inevitable crash into the stands ringing the area, before crouching low and sliding around at the last minute, using his hand as a pivot point. Jay's run was anything but routine. There were tricks, but they were spontaneous, unrehearsed and irreverent. He even tried some tricks he'd never tried before. Jay showed the world that skateboarding would no longer be defined by precisely executed handstands, coordinated routines and precise boundaries but by an expressive out-of-control desire to push the limits of what was possible on a piece of wood with four wheels beneath it.

At one point during his run, his hand on the ground, Adams slid his board right off the raised edge of the platform onto the ground below. The crowd went wild, not quite believing what they were seeing. Jay jumped back on the platform as if it was nothing and kept skating. Seconds later, he whipped out a 360 nose wheelie with his hand trailing along the ground, something that seemed to his friends to have just come to him in a fit of spontaneity. Next, as he tore across the platform, Jay grabbed his board with both hands, and like some caged monkey pulling madly on the metal bars of his prison, he bunny-hopped again and again, thrusting himself as high into the air as he could possibly go, until he ran out of speed. The older competitors shook their heads, the judges shook their heads, and the crowd was dumbstruck.

Over on the slalom course, the Zephyr team was likewise wrecking all pre-conceived limits and constraints that had ever been placed on the sport, but it was in the freestyle arena that the Dogtown style really made its mark. Jay's magic run was followed by equally impressive performances by other members of the team, including the lone Z-Girl, Peggy Oki, who ended up placing first in her class.

The Zephyr team disbanded soon after the contest—there were too many individuals among the Z-Boys for them to ever be a strong team. Over the following months and years, they continued to skate together and push the limits of the sport, even though they now rode for different companies.

After the team split up, former Z-Boys Jim Muir and Bob Biniak received a couple of pre-production skateboards from Tom Sims, who was working on developing stronger and lighter boards using laminates. For cost reasons, Tom decided not to mass-produce the boards, even though Jim and Bob were enthusiastic about them. So Jim decided to try making his own laminated skateboards, and Dogtown skateboards was born. Jim's friend Wes Humpston designed the graphics for the hand-crafted boards. Many of the best skateboarders of the time rode for Dogtown skateboards, including Tony Alva and a young Tony Hawk.

Over the course of the '70s, skating continued to grow at a crazy pace. In May 1975, an issue of *Skateboarder* came out with a photograph on the cover of a barefoot, blond kid named Greg Weaver, aka "the Cadillac Kid," carving halfway up the vertical wall of an empty pool.

"We all freaked!" remembers former Z-Boy Wentzle Ruml in an interview. "We were already buzzing tile and getting backside axle grinds, and here's this guy on the cover of the mag with the tile four feet above his head!"

By that time, the Dogtown crew was already hard at it, driving around searching for empty pools to carve up for as long as they could before getting kicked out.

"Pool riding is the state-of-the-art skating style of the '70s. No other type of riding offers such radical departure from the past," insisted an article that appeared in *Skateboarder* the following year. The article was right. Everybody who had ridden a pool knew that it was the future of skateboarding.

The former Z-Boys began to focus all their energy on skating pools, with Tony Alva and Shogo Kubo leading the way. Shogo was in his element carving the vertical walls of pools. He was one of the first skateboarders to express an appreciation for the aggressive chaos of pool lines that set vertical skating apart from the choreographed runs winning freestyle competitions and the straight-ahead speed and control needed to win in slalom or downhill.

"When I'm in a bowl, I just have to go for it," he told *Skateboarder* magazine in 1977. "It is not a routine that can be practiced, as only the first move can be planned." Shogo was a master of vertical improvisation. Even if one of his feet came off his board, he would find a way to stay on and finish his run without falling. When pools became the favored venue for skateboard contests in the late 1970s, Shogo was a contender. His aggressive carving style is plainly evident in many photographs from the era.

Soon, pools were "it," no question. Skateboarders everywhere began seeking out empty backyard pools wherever and whenever they could, sneaking in sessions, getting kicked out, running away from irate homeowners and the police and driving up and down alleys with one person standing on the roof of the van looking over fences for skateable backyard depressions. A drought was in full effect during the mid-1970s in Los Angeles, and water-use restrictions meant many pools were left empty. It was easy pickings.

When they found a good pool, lookouts squatted in the trees as the skaters carved up private property, wrecking edges, tiles, lights and elbows. The action was in the pool, down the alley, into a waiting car and off to the next pool. As soon as the young prodigies figured out how to carve the vertical walls, they were hooked.

Craig Stecyk, one of the founding fathers of the Zephyr surf shop, was an artist by trade. His photographs and articles for *Skateboarder* magazine came to define what the Z-Boys era of skateboarding was all about. Right away, Stecyk cottoned on to the "us and them" attitude of his tribe and began to nurture it. Skateboarding was no longer just something you did for fun. It was becoming something that defined who you were.

"Most people probably won't understand some of this, but that really doesn't matter since the intrinsic elements of this discussion are meant for those who really skate (just owning a skateboard or the old 'I was into it 10 years ago, so I understand it now,' doesn't qualify one as a skater)," Stecyk wrote in the introduction to an article he wrote for the fall 1975 issue of *Skateboarder*. "Modern skateboarding is a constantly evolving hybrid very few comprehend."

In the article, Stecyk insisted there were no limits to where skateboarding was headed. Everything that had come before was no longer applicable. Skateboarding was progressing at an impossible speed. The only restrictions the sport had were those of the skaters' own imaginations.

One day, Z-Boys Stacy Peralta, Tony Alva and Bob Biniak were skating one of their favorite spots, a giant of a pool in Beverly Hills known as the Keyhole Pool. A debate erupted between Peralta and Biniak over whether or not it was possible to do a frontside kickturn (turning 180 degrees with the front of your body facing the pool deck) on the vertical wall of the pool. The trick, commonplace nowadays, had never been done before. Stacy insisted it was possible, though he wasn't willing to be the first to try it. Bob refused to try it, saying it was impossible.

Two days later, the friends returned to the pool, and the debate flared up once again. Now Peralta was convinced his friend could pull it off. He jumped out of the pool onto the deck and began to egg him on. Finally, Biniak gave it a shot. He didn't make it, but he didn't give up. The next time he got closer but still didn't land it. On the third try, something clicked, and he came around and rode his board back down into the bottom of the pool.

"By the end of that day he was hitting frontside kickturns on tile," Peralta wrote in an article in *Thrasher* magazine. "This was a total breakthrough—an absolutely mind-blowing event. We went to the Keyhole that day for a session, just to skate, and Biniak ended up opening a new door."

A few months later, Stacy himself would be ripping frontside carves over the light and showing the world it was possible to do frontside kickturns over and over on the opposing vertical walls of a pool, a move known at that time as a frontside forever. It was beginning to look like Craig Stecyk was right when he said the only thing standing in the skaters' way was the limits of their own imaginations.

Tony Alva, like his friend Jay Adams, was a standout skater from the beginning. He had been skating the schoolyard banks since the late 1960s, honing his style with the old guard, guys like Torger Johnston, Danny Bearer and the Hilton brothers, who had pushed skating as far as it could go on clay wheels.

In other words, by the time urethane wheels came along, young Alva was already a force to be reckoned with. The Z-Boys exploded into the spotlight at the Del Mar contest in 1975 with Jay Adams' freestyle routine, but it was Tony Alva who eventually emerged to lead skateboarding into the future. His brash personality, his unshakeable will to succeed and his awesome skating ability made him the one to watch. The editors of *Skateboarder* couldn't help but notice his noisy entrance into the world of professional skateboarding. In the introduction to his first interview for the magazine in 1977, they wrote, "Tony Alva is the one skater today with the across-the-board appeal to surpass the boundaries of the skateboard sport/art."

His fellow skaters, including slalom and downhill legend Henry Hester, agreed. "Tony is just an insane rider. That's all there is to it," Hester told

Skateboarder. "He's the best skater in the world, probably, and he can do slalom too."

Alva effortlessly dominated almost every contest he entered, no matter what discipline it happened to be in. The frizzy-haired lunatic was so confident of his ability on a board that he set the world record for barrel jumping (leaping off a board over barrels and landing on another board) without even practicing for the event. In 1977, when he was 19 years old, Alva won the World Overall Professional Title.

Ripping around Los Angeles looking for pools to destroy, winning contests and living like a rock star was Tony Alva's life during those years. He traveled the world spreading the gospel of skateboarding, he started his own skateboard company and he even starred in a long-forgotten movie for Universal Pictures, imaginatively titled *Skateboard*.

Tony was living the life; he was on top of the world. He hardly needed to keep pushing himself in skateboarding. Still, it was his prerogative. Born with the same kind of relentless energy possessed by his partner in crime Jay Adams, he had no choice but to keep going and going, until one day he rolled into the Dog Bowl, a pool heavily sessioned by the original Z-Boys and their friends, grabbed his board and shot straight up into the air over the deck. Then, instead of bailing out, as any lesser mortal might have done, Alva slammed his wheels back onto the transition and raced back down into the bowl. It didn't seem possible. So he did it again. And again, and again, and again, until he had established the fact it was possible to ride your board up the vertical wall of a pool, into the air and back down again. The sport was officially introduced to the next level. When he was interviewed about the first skateboard aerials in *Skateboarder*, Alva, in his typical fashion, laid claim to the development outright.

"I was the first one to hit coping and then pull 'em up; I don't care what anyone else says," he told *Skateboarder* in his second interview in 1978. "You can ask Kent Senatore and Valdez and those guys, any of the guys that skated the Dog Bowl. I was the first one to use the coping as a launching trip to lift me up and out. When I do an aerial, I don't just go up and pull the board off the wall. I go up and *out off the wall*, then just drop back down. I'm trying to do 360 helicopter aerials out of the pool and backside 360s and stuff. I haven't seen anybody do that."

It would be a few years before anyone actually landed a 360 aerial, but the game was definitely on as soon as Alva first grabbed his board, shot into the air above the pool and reentered seemingly without effort.

Chapter Four

Unsung Heros of the 1970s

Russ Howell was a muscular, mustachioed 5' 3" powerhouse who dominated the freestyle skateboarding scene in the 1970s. With his gymnastic, stylized, choreographed routines, Russ Howell was the man to beat in the freestyle arena. Who else could perform jumps while doing a handstand, or do three-fingered handstands? Howell had a reputation as a fierce competitor with a single-minded dedication to his style of skating.

"I remember competing in my hometown at the Long Beach World Contest," he recalled in an interview. "Many of my friends were there, and I didn't want to disappoint them. My nerves were going crazy as I walked out onto the floor. I yelled at the top of my lungs, and the entire arena went silent. It helped. I wasn't thinking about my skating anymore."

Howell took his skateboarding seriously, frequently practicing up to 10 hours a day before competitions, but it wasn't always so. He started skateboarding for fun way back in 1958, when he was nine years old, but he didn't compete for the first time until the 1970s. While studying physical education, he was actually talked into competing by one of the kids at his local park where he had volunteered to help teach skateboarding.

Before long, "Grandpa Russ," as he was jokingly called by his envious fellow competitors, was chalking up victory after victory. In 1975, Howell earned the title of U.S. National Freestyle Champion. Two years later, he earned the world record for most consecutive 360s, with 163 spins.

Hailing from northern California, Kim Cespedes was one of the top female skaters of the late 1970s. She skated with a style strongly influenced by the Dogtowners—improvised and aggressive. She had the reputation of being among the first women to kickturn on steep walls and one of the only women able to powerslide at speed. As Brian Gillogly wrote in *Skateboarder*, "Kim thrives on full-bore, spontaneous bank and pool riding."

In the 1970s, Tom Inouye, known to his friends as Wally, was a dedicated all-around skateboarder, excelling in both freestyle and vertical. A photograph in the July 1977 issue of *Skateboarder* by famed Dogtown photographer Glen E. Friedman shows Tom pulling one of the first-ever backside airs at the grand opening of the SkaterCross Skatepark in Reseda, California. "Wally, reputedly, is one of the only skaters that the Dogtown boys consider to be really hot," wrote Curtis Hesselgrave in *Skateboarder*.

Ellen Oneal personified the choreographed, upright style of freestyle skateboarding, with its wheelies, walk the dogs and handstands, in the 1970s. Five years of ballet and a year of gymnastics training made it easy for Ellen to dazzle crowds with her smooth skating, flowing from maneuver to maneuver. Two-board trickery and nose wheelies at speed with two feet on the nose were no problem for Ellen, who starred alongside Tony Alva in the first feature-length skateboarding movie, *Skateboard*.

As one writer for *Skateboarder* put it, "Ellen's upright posture and graceful movements indicate an unassuming sense of pride and, as many observers have remarked, a bright future ahead in skateboarding." Skateboarding, unfortunately, had other plans, none of which involved upright, graceful movements.

Henry Hester, or "White Lightning," as his competitors called him, was an unbeatable force in slalom and downhill during the 1970s skateboarding boom. Hester dominated the competition, winning the Hang Ten World Championships twice and sharing a speed record at the infamous Signal Hill site of 57 miles per hour in a skate car. Hester's signature first-out-of-the-gate starts won him many duel slalom contests. As bowl and pool riding became more popular, Henry started competing in that as well, placing near the top of the heap, a testament to his ability to skate all types of terrain.

When his own skateboarding career began to slow down, Henry started the Hester Series, the first-ever pro bowl and pool riding competitions.

Chapter Five

Alan's Ollie

By 1977, Stacy Peralta was an international skateboarding superstar. He had won numerous contests, and his sponsors had flown him all over the world—Europe, the West Indies and Australia—to show the world how skateboarding was done in California. The amicable youngster was the poster boy for skating, appearing in *Freewheelin'*, a 35 mm film about skateboarding, and even making a cameo in the popular television show *Charlie's Angels*.

During the summer of '77, the straw-haired wonder boy set off on a tour of the East Coast with fellow skaters Greg Weaver and Wally Inouye and *Skateboarder* magazine photographer Warren Bolster. Their goal: to skate and photograph as many parks as they could from Maine to Florida. Presumably, they also wanted to show the East Coast skateboard crowd how far ahead the growing sport of skateboarding was in California.

Three years previous, in 1974, an 11-year-old kid from Florida named Alan "Ollie" Gelfand got his first skateboard. He was hooked right away, skating whenever and wherever he could. Before long, Alan had all the tricks dialed in and began inventing his own. One day, when he was at his local skatepark in Hollywood, Florida, Alan was practicing lipslides (a lipslide is when a skater slides the lip of a pool or a rail by first getting his back wheels over the lip to land facing the opposite way) on a sketchy part of the pool run where the lip extended past vertical, when he somehow managed to guide his board up into the air with his feet, turn it around and land back on the transition. The first time was a fluke, but he tried it again, and again it worked.

Alan began trying his new trick in different parts of the park where the lip didn't extend past vertical. Before long, he figured out how to kick the tail of his board against the concrete lip, thus bringing the board up to his feet so he could land back on it every time. His friends were flabbergasted. To honor their friend's invention, they began to call the trick an "ollie."

Peralta and his crew showed up at the skatepark in nearby Fort Lauderdale on the fifth day of their East Coast tour. Presumably, Alan had heard that the Californians were coming to town, because he was there, ready to skate. Stacy and the boys proceeded to rip around the skatepark, making the best of the shoddy bowls and rough snake runs and paying little heed to the scruffy youngsters skating around them, trying to get a piece of the action. Then something completely unexpected happened.

Stacy was taking a short break from skating when a local kid ran over, obviously excited. "Hey, you've gotta come and see this," he shouted at Stacy, gesturing toward the far side of the park. Curious, Stacy made his way over to where the skater was pointing. At first, as he remembers it, he was unimpressed with what he saw.

"Standing alone atop the three-foot cement bowl was a small Jewish kid skating in long pants. He looked out of place. No one skated in pants back then. No one."

Alan dropped in. Stacy watched as he rolled across the bowl and climbed up the opposing wall. Then, when Alan reached the lip, he snapped the tail of his board on the cement and flew into the air, his board glued to his feet as if by some magic force. Before Stacy could figure out what was going on, Alan had turned his board 180 degrees and landed back in the bowl.

"I was dumbfounded," Stacy remembers. "It happened so fast. I wasn't sure what I'd seen and thought for a moment that it was some kind of an illusion."

Stacy peered at little Alan's torn sneakers, assuming they were to blame for the miracle he'd just seen. "Can you do it again?" Stacy asked. Without a word, Alan dropped back into the bowl and ollied off the far wall.

Alan was a pint-sized teenager with little or no fashion sense skating in Florida, far from the center of skateboarding on America's West Coast. Still, Stacy had enough foresight to realize that what Alan was able to do with his skateboard threatened to change the sport of skateboarding forever. Mere months earlier, airs where you grabbed your board had seemed preposterous, and here was this kid doing no-hands airs! Stacy headed back to California to spread the word.

"Alan Gelfand. Man, he's heavy," Stacy told *Skateboarder* magazine in an interview later that year. "He's the perfect example of a guy doing something that people can't understand because it's so radical that people aren't going to be doing it for a long, long time. He's been doing this move called the ollie pop for two years, and people still aren't doing it like he does. He does aerials with no hands—ollie airs. Man, those things are insane."

The ollie would eventually become the most important trick in both vert and street skateboarding—the trick used to set up almost every other move invented since. And to think, it all started with a young kid just trying to figure out different ways to ride his skateboard somewhere in Florida.

Chapter Six

Powell Meets Peralta

George Powell had been a skateboarder since the mid-1950s, when he made his first board with a two-by-four and some old steel roller skate wheels. George eventually took enough time off from sidewalk surfing to earn an engineering degree from Stanford University. After graduating, he got a job working for an aerospace company, and when skateboarding resurfaced in the 1970s, he became excited about the possibility of designing and producing his own boards and wheels.

George bought some premixed urethane and began making his own wheels in his oven at home. He also started experimenting with various materials to use for boards. With the help and encouragement of legendary skateboarder Tom Sims, George invented a flexible board using aircraft aluminum around a maple core. The board was designed to compete with the most popular slalom board of the time, the Gordon & Smith Fibreflex.

The G&S Fibreflex boards, made from fiberglass and wood, were popular with slalom skateboarders in the 1960s. The surf company began reissuing them 10 years later, and they became one of the hottest boards once again. To capitalize on their success, G&S issued other Fibreflex boards designed for bowl riding and freestyle, and they eventually released an all-wood board called the Stacy Peralta Warptail model.

The Warptail flew off the shelves, with 110,000 boards sold in less than two years. With a $.50 commission from each board, Stacy was making money. Still, the sun-kissed Californian could see that it was getting crowded at the top and that the sun was eventually going to set on his career as a pro. He decided to diversify before it was too late.

"I didn't know if I was capable of doing anything," he said during an interview with skateboard.com. "I thought a lot about it, you know, what did I want to do. I wanted to create a great skateboard team, I wanted to put together really neat advertisements and I wanted to make products that skateboarders could relate to."

Meanwhile, in Santa Barbara, California, George Powell had been laid off from the aerospace company and was busy perfecting his skateboard wheels and producing more and more boards. After he produced several different models with Tom Sims, their partnership fizzled, and Powell went into business by himself. In 1977, he came up with a formula for urethane wheels that is still the standard today, and soon his Bones wheels were the best in the business.

Stacy approached George about the idea of forming a partnership. Stacy was one of the biggest names in skateboarding at the time, so it was a no-brainer for George, and in 1978, Powell Peralta skateboards was born. Stacy had no idea at the time that his abilities on the business end of skateboarding would outshine even his most radical moves on a board, and that the team he would form for his new company would become the most famous skateboard team in the history of the sport—the Bones Brigade. But that's a story for another chapter.

Chapter Seven

Vert Punks Rule!

The parks enabled a lot of skaters to come from their respective areas to meet and compete. It was this diverse make-up of different locales and ethnic backgrounds/upbringings that bore the fruit of what was to become the skate punk explosion.

–Steve Alba

Steve Alba, or "Salba" as he later became known, was a little '70s kid who lived to skateboard, carving around empty soda cans, jumping over broomsticks, doing nose wheelies and riding banks wherever he could find them. He and his friends had found a common bond that held them together and set them apart from all the rest of the kids at their school.

When the first 1970s issues of *Skateboarder* came out with pictures of the top riders carving the walls and lips of pools, Steve and his friends immediately set out to find some vertical walls of their own to ride. They rode numerous pools in and around their inland Southern California neighborhood. Soon the Badlanders, as they came to be known, were creating their own rules for skating pools and getting radical.

The growing popularity of vertical skateboarding led to a massive boom in skateboard park construction in the late 1970s. Parks began popping up all over the place, including near Steve's home. When the Pipeline skatepark opened in nearby Upland, Steve and his friends became instant locals. The park featured a massive double pool, called the Combi-pool, and a full pipe, modeled on the nearby Mt. Baldy drainage pipe, a legendary skate spot. As Steve says, Pipeline was the park that separated the men from the boys.

Thanks to new concrete skateparks like Pipeline, where skateboarders could practice airs and tricks for hours without getting interrupted by the police, skating was getting more difficult and aggressive. That suited Steve fine. He didn't mind wrecking his body to learn the latest lines. "Everything we did was done by trial and error," he recalls. "Pain was everywhere, but you learned to deal with it."

Steve watched and learned from the older Badlanders, and before long he was getting noticed, picking up sponsors and holding his own at any session or contest. Steve competed as an amateur in the ASPO (Association of Skate Park Owners) contests, and in the spring 1978, when he was 15, he turned pro. Steve won the first Hester Series bowl-riding contest in the spring of 1978, at Spring Valley skatepark, and he did decently at the next edition, held at Upland. Although he didn't finish in the top 10 at the third Hester bowl-riding contest at Newark skatepark, that day was a defining one for Steve, and indeed, for the whole sport of skateboarding.

"If you hung your head over the fence of the Newark keyhole pool that day, you could just feel things begin to change," Bob Denike wrote in the Independent Truck company's history of skateboarding, *Built to Grind*.

That day at Newark, two shady-looking characters, Fausto Vitello and Eric Novak, attended the contest and started giving away new skateboard trucks from the trunk of their car. From that day forward, Independent Trucks set the standard in truck design, and the company's take-no-prisoners attitude defined skateboarding culture.

Vitello and Noval approached Steve Alba and some other top skaters at the contest and asked if they would take their trucks for a test drive. After some deliberation, Steve agreed to give the trucks a shot. "I loved Indy trucks in that first half hour," he remembers. "I could turn so well, I was pulling figure-eight carves in the bowl. Nobody else could actually carve the bowl like that without lifting up their front wheels."

Up until then, Bennett, Tracker and Gullwing trucks had dominated the marketplace, but their designs still limited skateboarder's abilities to turn on vertical walls while enjoying a stable ride. When Independent came to Newark, they broke into the market with a formula nobody could argue with—their trucks simply worked better.

Steve made the finals in the pool-riding contest that day at Newark and placed second in the longest-carve contest with a monster wall burn over 13 feet long. Bobby Valdez also rode prototype Indys that day. He went on to win the bowl contest, narrowly beating out another new Indy rider named Rick Blackhart. Rick, a hardcore pool rider from San Jose, pulled the first-ever frontside roll-in (rolling along the deck with your back to the empty pool before dropping straight in over the lip) during his contest run. "I knew I had to do something that no one else was doing," he said, recalling how he learned to do the trick earlier the same morning in a nearby pool.

Rick Blackhart's improvisational power skating always wowed the crowds. Nobody was ever certain he was going to survive his run.

"I remember guys saying, 'He can almost eat s**t and make something out of it and keep going,'" Rick told Bob Denike during an interview. "The judges didn't catch onto that; the skating was too hard to judge 'cause it was different every time, but that's how I skated."

Blackhart was arguably the most hardcore skater of the time, and as the main test rider for Independent trucks, he contributed more to skateboarding than gnarly moves. As Fausto Vitello explained, Rick's mandate was to help design better skateboarding equipment, since in his opinion, all the equipment being manufactured at the time was garbage.

With typical flair, Rick turned down the offer of a limited partnership in the company, instead agreeing to test the trucks in exchange for $200 and a case of beer. Fausto Vitello and Eric Swenson built trucks, Rick took them for a little ride and told them what was wrong with them and how to improve them. Eventually, they got it right. "If you make these trucks, everyone will ride them," Rick told them. So they did, and people did.

Rick Blackhart embodied the skateboarding spirit of the day: go for broke and pay for it later. He also realized that Independent trucks would make it possible for him to skate like that with a slightly better chance of staying on his board.

Dave Dominy, one of the partners behind Tracker Trucks (arguably the most popular brand before the arrival of Independent), admitted that what Independent brought to that contest was the next step in truck design. "There is no question in my mind that the truck's success stems from how it feels when you ride it. If it didn't feel good, it probably wouldn't be here today," he told writer Bob Denike in an interview for *Built to Grind*. The aura of danger surrounding Independent's founders, and later their riders, was also key to the company's success.

"Independent came on like an electrical storm— low and buzzing," Bob wrote. "It seemed suddenly to have always been there, rolling in like a slow fog, creeping into skateboarding when something dark just felt necessary. It felt like the color black. It was dirty, leathery and raw. It felt illegal and greasy."

Soon, the Independent Truck logo, a rounded Maltese cross, was plastered everywhere, and the team was the dominating force both in bowl riding and racing. Independent went on to pick up Duane Peters and Steve Olson, two bowl skaters who would come to define what skateboarding was all about: punk attitude and uncompromising aggression.

Steve Olson, 1978's Skater of the Year, started skating as a teenager in 1966 on a steel-wheeled Roller Derby board. First, he was just bombing hills and cruising around the neighborhood, but after seeing a clip of skaters riding a pool in a surfing movie, Olson and his friends went out to find their own empty pools to skate. After signing with Santa Cruz and Independent Trucks, Olson became an uncompromising punk force in skateboarding's vertical phase. He dominated the Hester Series in 1978 with his ability to show up at any bowl or pool and destroy it, even if he'd never skated it before. "Bulky," as his friends called him, had coordination, strength and the imagination to more than hold his own as skateboarding became more daring and aggressive. A member of the original test team for Independent trucks and a founding team member of Santa-Cruz skateboards, Steve Olson set the standard for young skaters everywhere. He embodied the new style and attitude that was to dominate skateboarding over the coming years.

If Steve Olson was skate punk personified, Duane Peters was his protegé. Eric Swenson and Fausto Vitello had the sense to realize that Duane was the kind of no-holds-barred skateboarder that would be the perfect poster child for their company, so they signed him to Independent Trucks. Shortly after, Duane quit Dogtown to ride for Santa-Cruz. "We had the punkest team and absolutely tormented anybody who got in the way," Duane remembers.

Among other firsts, Duane, whose nickname was the "Master of Disaster," is credited with being the first skateboarder to "acid drop" into a pool (riding straight off the edge and landing at the bottom of the transitioned wall) and inventing the Indy air, named after his sponsor. The Indy is a backside air (meaning your backside is facing the edge of the pool) done while grabbing the toeside of your board between your feet.

By the next Hester Series contest at the Big-O skatepark, the Independent shadow fell long over its competition. Salba dominated, cementing his reputation as a force in the sport. Earlier that year, after he won the first contest of the series, other skaters doubted his abilities. He showed them that day at the Big-O.

"Everybody in the skate world told me that I was a fluke, but I came back hard and won with frontside airs and backside airs, channel airs, slides, bert reverts and roll-ins that I learned from Blackhart. Those were the raddest times for sure."

Santa-Cruz skateboards, an affiliate of Independent trucks, picked up most of the gnarliest riders of the time, including Salba, Duane Peters and Steve Olson. Olson was crowned the overall winner of the Hester Series. He was into punk rock, and his influence spread. Soon everyone, including Steve Alba, was cutting their hair, listening to punk rock, dressing like punks and acting like punks. The Santa Cruz/Independent punk rock contingent was too much for their competition to bear.

By the late 1970s, skateparks were everywhere, boards were wider and stronger, trucks were turning better, wheels were rolling smoother than ever and vertical skateboarding was progressing faster than most people could ever have imagined it would. Salba and Steve Olson were flying frontside airs right over the skatepark channels (gaps in the walls of pools allowing you to roll into the bottom). The channels had originally been designed to provide safe access to the pools, but now they were defining who had the most radical airs. The skaters even began catching air right over their friends carving turns below them on the vertical walls. Skating had become an aggressive sport dominated by a select few hardcore riders. *Skateboarder* magazine encouraged the sport's change in direction, dropping most of its coverage of slalom, downhill and freestyle competitions and focusing almost exclusively on pool-riding events. There's no room for pretenders anymore, seemed to be the prevailing attitude, and a lot of skaters, feeling alienated by the hardcore direction the sport was taking, simply gave up. Others, such as Doug "Pineapple" Saladino, tried to keep up with the leading edge for as long as they could and continued to push the sport.

In the mid-1970s, Doug was a little kid from San Diego competing against skateboarding giants, but by age 13, he was becoming a giant himself, placing near the top of the field in pro freestyle contests and occasionally even winning. By the end of the decade, he had jumped on the vert-riding bandwagon and became one of the best pool riders out there. Pineapple was the first Independent Trucks rider from southernmost California.

Salba's younger brother Micke (also known as Malba) was another ripper who began blowing minds at an early age, turning pro for Kryptonics at the tender age of 12. Malba learned to skate riding the super-deep Combi-Pool at the Pipeline skatepark and the Mt. Baldy Pipeline full pipe nearby. During skateboarding's dark days in the early 1980s, Micke and his brother refined the art of pool skating at impossible speeds.

Another heavy skater at the time was Steve Cathey, whose motto was, "If you snooze, you lose." Throughout skating's boom in the 1970s, Steve was rarely caught napping. Having his picture taken by legendary skateboard photographer Warren Bolster and published in *Skateboarder* when he was 15 gave Steve the boost he needed to become a serious competitive skater. He would force himself to practice for hours until he learned every trick he ever saw anyone complete.

Steve was a strong contender in the Hester-ISA Pro Bowl Series. Whether he was carving the vertical walls of his favorite skatepark to the tunes of a Ted Nugent rocker or rolling through a smooth-as-silk freestyle routine to the strains of Steve Miller, Steve Cathey was one to watch. He became one of the most prominent faces in skateboarding, appearing in movies, newspaper and magazine articles, print advertisements and TV commercials promoting his sport or endorsing a product.

In the late 1970s, skating was changing fast, and Steve was definitely one of the last of the old guard, a skater whose smooth style was influenced by his days surfing California's shore breaks. In a 1978 issue of *Skateboarder,* he explained the difference between his skating and that of a much younger team member, up-and-comer Dennis Martinez. "The way you skate is the way you skate," he said. "There's being smooth and then there's more of a radical style such as Dennis has. I really dig the way he skates. Me and Dennis can go for a frontside grinder, but our approach is different. He has a really radical, aggressive style and I'm more casual. When I skate a pool, though, I really like to attack it and be aggressive, but I don't go for the full-on body torque and gnarly face expressions. I guess that's why I seem much more mellow and make it look easier."

By the end of the 1970s, skateparks, some of which had just opened months earlier, were suffering major financial losses. Opportunist operators were losing money hand over fist thanks to lousy designs, high insurance costs, lawsuits from angry parents and skateboarding's marginalizing of the other aspects of the sport. Parks began to close, and skateboarding went underground almost overnight.

By the time the first issue of *Thrasher* came out in January 1981, it was clear to everyone that skateboarding needed some fresh input and a new attitude.

"I often feel that skateboarding has painted itself into a curious corner," wrote *Thrasher* editor Kevin Thatcher in his first editorial for the new magazine. "It is almost its own worst enemy in that it has become over overspecialized—almost elitist in attitude."

The editorial served as a call to arms, a plea to skaters everywhere to forget about what they saw in the magazines, forget about trying to emulate their heroes. Just get out there and skate.

"Skateboarding has not yet reached its maximum potential, and who can say what the limits are?" Kevin asked the world. "To find out, grab that board!"

Chapter Eight

Enter the Bones Brigade

In an era of specialization, the Bones Brigade is a diversified force. Specialization breeds stagnation, while functional evolution leads to survival. The future requires creative adaptability.

–Bones Brigade ad. 1981

Stacy Peralta signed on with George Powell and went straight to work assembling the Powell Peralta team. Stacy drafted some of the best skateboarders of the time, all with their own distinct style—guys like Jay Adams, Alan Gelfand, Ray "Bones" Rodriguez (who had ridden for George's wheel company) and Scott Foss. Showing the sort of vision he became famous for, Stacy also signed two other upstarts, Stevie Caballero and Mike McGill. In no time, the Bones Brigade was the team to watch.

The Bones Brigade team represented the new direction skateboarding was taking, with a strong emphasis placed on vert riding and progression but with a nod to the emerging reality of skateboarding happening anywhere at anytime.

For two years, through skateboarding's darkest days, Stacy kept on working to build the ultimate team, making sure his skaters were at the top of their game. In 1980, Steve "Cab" Caballero became the hottest skater in the world overnight when he landed the first-ever 360 aerial at the Gold Cup Finals at the Pipeline skatepark, launching off the lip backward, grabbing his board and bringing it around to re-enter the transition frontward. The move was named the Caballarial.

The list of skaters at that contest reads like a who's who of legends from both the aggressive bowl-carving era of the late 1970s and the technical vert-riding era of the 1980s. The Variflex team, with trick wizard Eddie Elguera at the helm, was there. Micke and Steve Alba were there, as were Duane Peters and future Bones Brigader Ray "Bones" Rodriguez. Future Brigaders Lance Mountain and Mike McGill were there, too. Basically, *everyone* was there to see a pint-sized kid named Steve Caballero take home the gold, wow the judges with his supreme board control and usher in the next phase of vertical skateboarding.

In his autobiography, Tony Hawk describes his impression of the older Caballero. "Steve wasn't simply a better skater than most, he was a natural innovator—exactly what I strove to be."

Almost as soon as he stepped on a skateboard for the first time in 1976, Steve Caballero had it figured out. By the time he was 13 years old, he was already a sponsored amateur, riding for Powell skateboards and placing well at contests. In 1980, while skating the 10-foot-deep keyhole pool at Winchester skatepark, he invented the famous trick that was named after him, the Caballarial.

Cab had learned every other trick being done at the time on vert, and he wanted to push it further. One day, while he and a friend were practicing fakie 360 kickturns (going up the wall backward, spinning once around and coming back down the wall forward), he got the idea to try popping off the lip to do a fakie ollie while spinning a 360. "I just started trying it, turning my body, and finally I did it," he told *Concrete Powder*.

The trick blew people's minds. As soon as they heard about it, they had to see it. When Cab's mentor and team manager, Stacy Peralta, saw it, he knew he'd made the right decision signing the young daredevil. That same year, at age 15, Caballero turned pro for Powell.

The Caballarial opened up a whole new dimension in vert skating. Spinning tricks were the future. Right away, Lance Mountain and Neil Blender tried to copy their friend's new trick, but they couldn't come close. Instead, they started grabbing their boards as they shot into the air for the spin. In this way, they came up with a grabbing variation of the Caballarial that, for reasons of their own, they decided to call the Gay Twist.

Steve was small of stature, but his skating packed a huge punch. It was obvious to anyone who saw him skate a ramp or a pool back in the early '80s that he would be among the group leading skateboarding's next charge. Sure enough, Steve set the record for the highest-ever backside air in 1987, blasting 11 feet out of the famous Raging Waters ramp in San Jose, California.

"Stevie was incredible, years ahead of other skaters," Tony Hawk wrote in his biography. "I though he was the most innovative skater at the time, and I doubt you could find anybody to argue with me."

"[Steve] skates smooth as ice, pumping through easy tricks like blood through a beating heart and taming tough tricks into pictures of perfection," writes Keith David Hamm in his book, *Scarred for Life*.

Like many of his Powell teammates, Steve skated hard through the early 1980s, when skateboarding was trying to find its new direction. He rose to fame in the latter half of the decade during the glory days of the Bones Brigade but stayed active in skateboarding long after that, effortlessly adapting his skating to the street.

The thrill of skateboarding is what drove him right from the start—the constant striving to do things others deemed impossible.

"Fear is good at times," he said during an interview with Thrasher. "It's a warning to tell you you're not ready to do this. But getting over fear means taking chances as well. If you never take a chance in life, you'll never overcome your fears."

In the early 1980s, with all the parks closing, it was getting harder and harder to find decent spots to skate, and it was becoming doubtful whether skateboarding was going to survive its biggest slump in 10 years. Thankfully for skateboarding, there were enough people to carry the torch, people like Stacy Peralta. All the while, Stacy kept working on his team, driving them to every contest he could find, doing tours, holding demos and showing the world that skateboarding was alive and well and becoming more radical every day.

Some of his riders, including Caballero (who was named rookie of the year in 1981) were proving themselves to be among the best innovators in the sport. Floridian freestyle phenom Rodney Mullen, the only freestyler on the team, was simply untouchable, inventing a seemingly endless series of tricks that no other skater could come close to performing.

At around the same time the Bones Brigade was taking shape, a young spaghetti-limbed brat from Tierrasanta, California, began learning how to skateboard. His name: Tony Hawk.

"I recognized that he was the future," wrote Rodney Mullen in his autobiography, recalling the first time he saw Tony Hawk skate. "You could spot his genius in seconds; he looked so fluid and relaxed, while other skaters seemed forced and unnatural on their boards. I couldn't believe that anyone could achieve such mastery as a skater...He was an extremely smart guy, and you could see that skating was an extension of his intelligence just by watching the way he learned a trick."

Tony Hawk was born with a surfeit of energy and determination. As a hyperactive, hyper-intelligent child, he drove his parents crazy. Luckily he found skateboarding, a sport that would absorb his energy completely and give it direction.

For the first few months, Tony's new skateboard was just another toy. He would ride it around the neighborhood with his friends but didn't think much of it. But as soon as he discovered nearby Oasis skatepark, his life changed drastically. The park became his second home, and with seemingly endless reserves of determination, Tony began to learn all the maneuvers he saw others doing there.

In December 1981, Stacy gave young Tony Hawk a call. The team manager had seen a spark in skateboarding's tiniest terror during a contest, and he wanted that spark on his team. The timing of Stacy's call couldn't have been better, since Tony's first sponsor, Dogtown, had just folded. The company that had risen from the ashes of the original Zephyr skateboard team could not weather skateboarding's slump. Tony joined the Bones Brigade as an amateur when he was only 12 years old.

As soon as he joined the Bones Brigade and started skating with his older heroes, Tony's skating went into overdrive. Suddenly, he wasn't just up against all the little kids in his age group—he was competing against the best skateboarders in the world.

The first skate contest that Tony traveled to with Stacy was in Jacksonville, Florida. "I couldn't have skated more terribly if I'd tried," he remembers. "I was so out of my element, it was brutal. Skaters from all over the country had congregated in Jacksonville, and skating was dead! If skating had actually been popular and I'd had to compete against more skaters, I think I would have cried after the contest." Although Tony continued to suck at contests, he kept right on skating—his ingrained determination would never let him quit. Besides, by that time he had bought wholeheartedly into the dead sport nobody wanted any part of. He skulked around his school, avoiding bullies and longing for the time when he could head back to the Del Mar Skate Ranch, the center of his existence.

When he was 14, Tony turned pro for Powell Peralta. The decision wasn't one he put much thought into, since there was little or no money for a professional in the sport at that time. That said, Tony placed third in his first contest as a pro. After that, he kept skating as much as he could, unafraid to slam his puny body into the bottom of the cement bowls, learning, progressing and fast becoming one of the best vertical skateboarders in the world, unbeknownst to himself. Then one day, he was surprised to see a photo of himself on the cover of *Thrasher* magazine. Soon after getting the cover, Tony won his second contest as a pro, at Del Mar. He had paid his dues—he was now among the best in the business.

The Bones Brigade was gaining momentum, and with skateparks everywhere closing down, skaters were taking matters into their own hands. They were building giant ramps in their backyards to fulfill their need to skate vert. More and more contests began taking place on giant half-pipes, and the ramp-riding style of skating that had more to do with back-to-back tricks than having the smoothest style became the norm.

In 1983, Bones Brigader Mike McGill invented a new trick while riding a ramp at a summer camp in Sweden. Mike unveiled the trick (basically an inverted 540-degree spin, one-and-a-half times around with a flip thrown in for good measure) during the last contest held at the Del Mar Skate Ranch. People were literally dumbstruck when he pulled it.

Skateboard writer Jocko Weyland was there, sitting in the bleachers when it happened. McGill rode up off the top of the pool and did a regular backside air, gaining speed for his next trick. When he reached the lip of the opposite wall, he shot about five feet up into the air, spinning around and around and upside down before landing frontward on the wall. Jocko and the rest of the crowd couldn't believe what they had just seen.

"As he came down, a collective gasp turned into a wail of astonishment," wrote Jocko, describing the event. "People lost it. There was a shared and unifying hysteria. Everybody howled. I howled along with them. In those hoarse yells was the agony and delirium of a severe cognitive break... A new dimension had opened up. The McTwist was a quantum leap out of the imagination into the real."

Jocko was not overstating the importance of this trick in the history of vertical skateboarding. It was, quite literally, the end of an era. Vertical skaters who had been hanging onto their fading careers quit in droves, while young, hungry upstarts like Tony Hawk went off by themselves to learn the trick they knew they had to conquer if they wanted to stay in the game.

Mike first joined the Bones Brigade in 1979. The young skater from Florida was part of the new breed of vert skaters who took a methodical approach to learning as many tricks as they could to win contests. Mike won his fair share of contests, too, but that's not what he will be remembered for. Skaters will always remember Mike as the guy who invented the McTwist.

The trick was actually first invented by roller skaters. When Mike saw roller skater Fred Blood pop out of the Egg Bowl at the Cherry Hill skatepark in New Jersey and spin around one-and-a-half times, he started trying to figure out how to do the same thing on his skateboard.

"At least two years had passed, and I found myself trying to do this crazy 540 thing with Caballero in a hotel swimming pool full of water," McGill wrote in *Thrasher*. "Of course he had no idea what I was doing. We mostly just tried contorted handplants in the shallow end as water went up our noses."

It wasn't until the end of the following summer that Mike gathered up enough courage to try the move on a ramp. He was in Sweden with fellow

Bones Brigaders Lance Mountain and Rodney Mullen, supposedly to help coach 40 or so young Swedish skaters into becoming the next vert heroes, but actually spending most of the time just skating.

Along with European skate legends Bod Boyle from England and Claus Crabke from Germany, Mike had been skating the same ramp for three weeks, every day, three sessions a day. By the time he decided to give the 540 a shot, he had pretty much landed every other trick he'd wanted to land. He decided to skip dinner, don some extra pads and land the trick he'd been thinking about for years.

Looking like a modern-day gladiator, with duct-taped wrist guards and two layers of padding on his hips, Mike headed out to the ramp.

"If I can just get past the 400-degree mark, I can bail out to my knees and not land on my head," he thought to himself. To do that, though, Mike knew he was going to have to go high and fast. The risk factor was elevated, but he knew the pay-off, should he land the trick, would make it all worthwhile.

Bod watched as the older American skater threw himself into the air before crashing down onto his knees on the transition over and over again. Then, after 20 or so tries, Mike shot into the air high over the ramp, spun one-and-a-half times around and came back down, landing perfectly in the curve of the ramp.

"No bloody way!" Bod screamed, before leaping to his feet and charging off toward the cafeteria to spread the word among the other campers.

After a short while, the sides of the ramp were crowded with spectators. Naturally, they didn't expect much different than what they had been seeing all summer. Maybe Mike would make it one-and-a-half times around, but he was probably going to spin halfway up the wall of the ramp, not in the air above it.

"Okay, let's see it," someone said, breaking the mood of tense expectation. Mike climbed up on the ramp and dropped in. After a couple of warm up airs, he tucked low and bombed across the flat bottom, winding his shoulders up slightly and preparing for the spin.

He launched off the coping and high into the air, grabbing his board "mute" (with his lead hand on the toe edge of his board). He spun hard, his body floating upside down as he torqued his shoulders to get around. He came around, still well above the ramp, with plenty of time to spot his landing.

"I was actually about four feet out, which made it easier for me to see what I was doing," he explained later. Mike smoothed his wheels down onto the curved wall of the ramp before shooting across to the other side. He popped up onto the opposite deck only for a second before the assembled skaters went nuts.

Mike went back to California, obviously excited to make a splash with his insane new trick. As Neil Blender recalled in *Thrasher,* nobody was expecting it. McGill's McTwist arrived in California like a massive, trembling earthquake, shaking the sport to its core.

"McGill shows up out of the blue, carves a few walls, does a few rocks, maybe a backside air or two, then you hear the crack of his tail ring out as he tumbles through the air," Neil remembered. "It was surreal; I freaked out like the time Cab unveiled the Caballarial at Marina years before."

"The move, to me, seemed too advanced to learn. To this day, when I see digital clocks at 5:40, I get a little nervous," Neil added. Neil wasn't the only one made nervous by the McTwist's sudden arrival on the scene. Many vert skaters decided it was a harbinger of more gnarliness to come, and maybe it was time to hang up the pads and take up golf.

"People were just walking away and taking off their pads—just walking away from the most heated session at the most important contest of the year," remembers 1980s pro skater Jeff Grosso in an amazing article about the trick in *Thrasher*. "We were all like zombies."

As Grosso remembers it, one other pro skater stepped up to the plate that day and knocked off a 540, proving to the world that the trick was no fluke. Lester Kasai was the skater's name, and he blasted a McTwist high and fast, spinning straight up into the air and coming back down almost exactly where he had taken off.

Many other skaters eventually learned the trick over the next few months, including Tony Hawk, Lance Mountain and an amazingly gifted youngster named Christian Hosoi, who almost eclipsed Mike McGill by going so high and spinning so slowly that he practically reinvented the trick. Others weren't so lucky. They'd try it over and over again, but committing to a 540 McTwist was not easy. It wasn't just a simple matter of determination; you had to have serious guts to pull this move off.

"All the while, kids would be chanting, 'Twist! Twist!'" Grosso remembers. "The 540 had become the it trick. If you didn't have it, you didn't have s**t."

Grosso himself eventually landed a McTwist, but it was long after the time when he was competing among skateboarding's best.

After two months of spending every waking hour either thinking about or practicing the McTwist,

Tony Hawk finally managed to land the trick. He remembers the feeling. "I was the happiest guy in the world. I could have rammed into the other wall and knocked my head off, and as I died, I'd have been wearing the biggest grin you'd ever seen."

With the arrival of the McTwist, Bones Brigader Lance Mountain was worried that skating was passing him by, but his determination to learn the trick showed he had the right attitude to stay in the game. He practically killed himself trying to land the difficult one-and-a-half spin, landing flat on his back in the middle of the ramp after pulling too hard off the wall.

Lance spent days trying to land the trick, smashing his board in frustration, setting up a new board, trying again, then smashing his board again. "I'd go out, put another board together, try it all day, just wimp out, smash my board up, throw it around and get all pissed off," he said. Finally Lance got sick of his own antics and decided he was going to land the trick once and for all. So he did. Lance claimed he didn't learn the seminal trick because he had to, but because he wanted to. Either way, the fact that he got the difficult trick so wired it actually became fun for him most definitely helped shape his future involvement in the sport.

Lance grew up skating sketchy ramps and sessioning the giant asphalt bank behind the local

Arby's restaurant near his home with his friends. When a skatepark opened up nearby in the LA suburb of Montebello, Lance and his posse learned to ride the concrete snake runs. At the time, vert skating was gaining strength, and Lance and his friends wanted to give it a try. They ended up building a half-pipe.

Lance's vert skating took off, and he was excited to show his parents how much he'd progressed. One day, he took them to a local backyard pool to watch him skate. Perhaps a little too eager to display his prowess, Lance dropped in and promptly knocked himself out. The incident led his parents to end the youngster's burgeoning skateboard career prematurely.

But parental controls couldn't stop Lance, and before long, he was back on his board trying to erase the reputation he'd built for himself as the kook who'd ruined it for everybody by forcing the closure of one of the most popular skate spots in the area.

Luckily, at that time, skateparks were popping up all over, and pools and bowls were everywhere. A helmeted Lance was soon proving himself to be among the best young vert riders. By the time he was 16, no one among his friends was as dedicated to skating as Lance. He was traveling all over to compete in contests and doing pretty well in them.

He met new friends who had the same sort of drive and ambition he had for skating—John Lucero, Neil Blender and Steve Caballero. In the summer of 1979, Lance won second place at his first amateur pool-riding contest at Lakewood Skatepark. He was on his way.

He competed in the popular ASPO contests for his local park, Whittier Skatepark, and in 1981, he picked up a sponsorship from Variflex, even though he really wanted to ride for Powell with his new friend Stevie. Lance finished second overall in the Gold Cup Series and then went on a U.S. tour with his new team.

"I think I was the only amateur ever to go on tour," he told *Transworld Skateboarding* during an interview. "That opportunity really convinced my parents that I had a future in skateboarding."

Unfortunately, over the following months skateboarding tried to erase itself completely from the public consciousness. Parks everywhere closed, skate companies went bankrupt, and people quit the sport in droves. Lance wasn't about to quit, but he had to reexamine where he was at in skateboarding. Lance tried working in the real world for a while, setting up tables at trade shows and silk screening boards at Variflex. He was bummed out. He'd dedicated years to skateboarding, but now he was burned-out on that, too. Before he had much time to think about his future prospects, he got the break he'd been waiting for. Lance got picked up by Stacy and became a member of the Bones Brigade.

Lance rode for Powell for over a year before being issued with his own pro model. At the time, he thought his career was winding down, and he didn't deserve to have his own model. Little did he know, he would become one of skating's most enduring icons, still active over 20 years later. Shortly after being sponsored by Powell, Lance won the Thanksgiving Day Turkey Shoot contest at the Pipeline Skatepark in Upland. Then the *Bones Brigade Video Show* came out. After his stellar performance in the video, he was granted a pro model, and it soon became one of the bestselling boards of all time.

Lance traveled the world with the Bones Brigade. He went to Italy, Denmark and Canada and attended the skateboard summer camp in Sweden where Mike McGill first learned the McTwist. "He did one over my head," Lance recalled in an early interview in *Transworld*. "I just cried and said, 'I've got to quit skating now. It's the worst. It's over with. Then I learned them. I just told myself that I had to learn them."

By 1985, skateboarding was on the upswing again, Lance was married with a child, and the Bones Brigade was the biggest team in the business. Throughout vertical skateboarding's glory days in the 1980s, Lance was at the forefront, killing it in competitions, in videos and in demos.

His tricks were insane, his board was everywhere and his name was on every skater's lips.

The last contest of 1983 was held at Upland Pipeline in the gnarly Combi-Pool. The Combi-Pool, the home turf of Badlanders Micke and Steve Alba, was the roughest and steepest of all the skatepark pools. Because of his diminutive stature and trick-based style of skating, Tony Hawk had yet to convince the skateboarding world that he was a contender, but he was determined to show them that he could skate the harsh walls of the Combi-Pool with the best of 'em. And he did. Ripping huge airs, and landing a flurry of complicated tricks, Tony ruled the pool, placing fourth behind his three teammates, Lance Mountain, Steve Caballero and Mike McGill. The Bones Brigade was now officially the dominating force in skateboarding.

Chapter Nine

Rodney Mullen: Untouchable

Rodney Mullen figured out how to ollie on the flat ground, and street skating wouldn't exist without the ollie...Rodney invented the kickflip. Ollie impossible? Rodney. Rodney, Rodney, Rodney.

–Tony Hawk

In a television clip from the early 1980s, an announcer at a freestyle skateboarding contest can be heard warning Rodney Mullen before his run, "You've gotta stay on top. You just don't *get* first place out here, just for coming out. You've gotta go out and do it for two minutes worth."

Of course, Rodney knows all this. He's gone over his run a million times in his head. He's practiced it a thousand times. For Rodney, it's automatic. When he starts skating, he's already assured himself that there will be no mistakes—his run, like all his other runs, will be perfect. Rodney is in complete control.

Freestyle skating contests of the time resembled figure skating routines. Skaters pulled off complicated footwork in time with the music, moving around the contest area with fluid motions synched with the sounds of 1980s new-wave bands. The cheese factor was just as high for Rodney as for everyone else, right down to his choreographed index finger salute—number one!—reserved for the pause after a particularly complicated trick.

The music kicks in, and Rodney goes to work, spinning multiple 360s effortlessly on his front wheels before reaching into his bottomless bag of shuv-it variations (spinning the board around beneath your feet without spinning your body), truckstands (flipping the board up and standing on the trucks) and handstand flips (standing on your hands on the board, then flipping the board along its length with your hands before landing back on it). Near the end of his run, he pulls an ollie impossible (flipping the board from end to end around the foot), a move no other skater could even dream of doing at that time. When his two minutes are up, Rodney skips off into the stands with a broad smile on his face. He's obviously happy that he was able to pull off another perfect run. But was there ever any doubt that he would?

Rodney Mullen's contribution to modern skateboarding is second to none. From the first day he stepped onto a friend's skateboard, Rodney was completely absorbed by the infinite creative possibilities it seemed to offer up.

"There wasn't really an established 'right' way to skate, no set rules as there are in baseball," he wrote in his autobiography, *The Mutt: How to Skateboard and Not Kill Yourself*. "Nothing in my life up until then had allowed such total creativity."

Unfortunately for Rodney, his father was a dentist who had already made up his mind about the dangers of skateboarding after repairing a kid's smashed teeth. There was no way he was going to allow his 10-year-old son to partake in this risky sport.

In spite of his father's objections, Rodney held on to his dream of one day becoming a skateboarder. Even though he had only ridden his friend's board a few times, he was consumed with the idea of skating, frequently visiting the local skateshop and memorizing the names of all the boards, imagining the day he'd finally be able to own one—if that day should ever come.

Finally, on New Year's Eve 1976, Rodney's father caved, and the next day, he took his son to buy his first skateboard. From that first day onward, Rodney spent every free minute practicing his skateboarding, focusing all his energy on learning new tricks.

Rodney learned how to do 360s, then four or five 360s in a row, and before long he was whipping 20 or 30 in a row outside of the Inland Surf Shop, near his home in Florida. Nine months after getting his board, Rodney picked up a sponsorship from the shop.

Shortly afterward, the shop owners entered him in a small, local freestyle contest, and he won. In his second contest, a much bigger event held at Kona Skatepark in Jacksonville, Florida, Rodney placed third in the amateur division and attracted the attention of Bruce Walker from Walker Skateboards. Walker became Rodney's first board sponsor.

Bruce and local skateshop owner Barry Zaritsky became Rodney's mentors. They saw the phenomenal talent developing and did everything they could to nurture it. Rodney won his third major contest, this time against sponsored skaters from all over Florida, and soon his desire to be the best freestyle skater out there began to consume him. Rodney's father was hard on his son, and didn't settle for second best. He expected his children, particularly Rodney, to rise to every occasion.

"I had absorbed my father's attitude toward goals, and after I won that contest I knew that if I fell behind I would only have myself to blame," he wrote.

Given Rodney's single-minded dedication to freestyle skating, his complete obsession with learning every possible trick in existence and his growing ability to make up his own moves, it's no surprise that he began to make a name for himself early on, even among the major-league skaters of the time. When Rodney entered a major contest at the Clearwater skatepark, he placed third behind top pro freestylers Tim Scroggs and Jim McCall. Rodney was surprised by his result, since he looked up to the pros of the time and never expected, as a 12-year-old, to be treated as one of their equals.

In 1979, Rodney went out to California with his sister to enter an amateur contest at the Oceanside skatepark. Not fully believing in his own talent yet, he entered himself in the 11–13 sponsored category. Naturally, he won by a huge margin. Over the next year, a lot happened in Rodney's life that would further drive him in skateboarding. First of all, his father told him he was wasting too much time with skateboarding, and he was going to have to stop before the beginning of the next school year. It seems absurd, but that's how things went in Rodney's family. Rodney's father was a controlling man who decided when and how his son was going to go about becoming successful in life.

"I had done everything I could to keep my skating from being taken away," Rodney wrote. "But it was no good. It was impossible. To him, skating had no future, and I was just dithering my life away."

Still, Rodney had the better part of a year to keep dithering away on his skateboard, and so he did with unparalleled zeal, skating a minimum of two hours every day during the week and 10 hours over the weekend.

That same year, Stacy Peralta contacted him. Peralta had seen him skate at Oceanside and knew Rodney was something special. So he offered Rodney the opportunity to come and skate at the biggest contest of the summer at Oasis Skatepark in San Diego, California.

Rodney went to the contest, skated better than any pro in attendance, including the inimitable Steve Rocco, and won. Nobody could match the hoard of new tricks Rodney had invented while skating alone in his parent's garage in Florida. In fact, Rodney was disappointed when he saw how slowly the rest of the skaters at the time were evolving.

"It bummed me out," he wrote in *The Mutt*. "I expected them to be on the fast track, learning new tricks twice or three times as fast as me." The only other competitor that impressed Rodney was Steve Rocco, and after the contest the two freestylers became friends.

Luckily for the skateboarding world, when Rodney returned to Florida with his trophy and some exciting stories to tell, his father reversed his decision once again. Rodney was allowed to continue to skateboard.

He returned to the sport with even more zeal, locking himself into strict practice schedules and regimenting his entire life around skateboard sessions. He turned pro for Powell and Peralta and started traveling more often to California and elsewhere for contests and demos as a valued member of the Bones Brigade.

It seems amazing now, but at that time even advanced freestylers like Rodney weren't doing ollies on the flatground. Of course, it was Rodney who finally figured it out, and when he did, a picture of him doing the trick appeared on the front cover of *Thrasher*.

Rodney was moving light years faster than any of his closest competitors. He learned how to ollie into flip tricks and invented the ollie kickflip—called the magic flip at the time, because nobody could figure out how he flipped his board. His dominance of freestyle skateboarding was total, but his father took exception with the way skateboarding was ruling his son's life. Rodney was quiet, non-confrontational and withdrawn by nature, but his dad blamed skateboarding for what he viewed as weakness in his son. He decided once again that his son would no longer be allowed to skate after that summer.

Once again, Rodney was overcome with worry, thinking about how he was going to survive without skateboarding, but he need not have worried so much. There was no way anyone, not even his own domineering father, could stop him from doing the thing that he loved most in life. A month after his second early retirement, Rodney was skating again. The following year, 1984, he re-entered competition, handily winning the National Skateboarding Association's World Open.

During the 1980s, freestylers were second-class citizens in the skateboarding world, their amazing skills on the flatground eclipsed by the high-flying bravado of the vert guys. That never bothered Rodney as he toiled away, refining his tricks and inventing new ones at an astonishing rate. Besides, as Stacy Peralta told him, freestyle skaters were valuable, since they could hold demos anywhere, thus acting as ambassadors for skateboarding in all sorts of venues.

When street skating started to gain popularity, however, things began to change on the contest landscape. The spontaneous, daring excitement of streetstyle contests eclipsed the measured finesse of freestyle. Street and vert pros were ruling the skate scene, and nobody cared about freestyling anymore.

The freestyle event at the third edition of the Savannah Slamma in 1989 happened far away from the massive indoor arena where the street contest was held. While skateboarding's bad boys Christian Hosoi, Jeff Kendall, Eric Dressen, Mark Gonzales, Lester Kasai and emerging young phenom Danny Way were killing the street course in front of a giant crowd down at the arena, Rodney and his freestyle comrades were flipping their boards for nobody on a rough patch of asphalt at the end of a cul-de-sac.

Thrasher writer Miles tried his best to inject some excitement into his recollection of the event. "Rodney proved that he still exists on a different gravitational plane than anyone else. A handstand 180 and ollie grabs higher than your belly button were but a couple of his magical stunts," he wrote. "The five highest scorers from both heats skated in a final jam. The crowd moved closer, the skaters let loose with more skippin', flippin' and flapdoodlin' and the end results were Grogan, Brown, Andre, Welinder and the always unbeatable Mr. Mullen."

Rodney ruled the world of freestyle skateboarding, but sadly, nobody cared anymore. Eventually, freestyle skateboarding contests were replaced by demos, and the only venue for the likes of Rodney was as a sort of goofy half-time exhibit. It took Rodney a while to realize he needed to take his amazing skateboarding ability to the streets, but he eventually figured it out, largely thanks to the support of his two friends Steve Rocco and Mike Ternasky, the two people who picked up on where skateboarding was going at the end of the 1980s.

Chapter Ten

Straight to Video

At the end of 1983, Stacy Peralta finished production of the *Bones Brigade Video Show*. At first, a neighbor approached Stacy with the idea for a skate video, but in the end, Stacy simply bought the equipment and made the video himself.

He shot about 100 hours of footage over eight months, and using a tape-to-tape editing system in his apartment, Stacy cut the movie himself before premiering it in Tony Hawk's parent's living room in the spring of 1984. The *Bones Brigade Video Show* was the first action sports video of its kind. It was designed to promote the Powell Peralta brand, which it did, causing a giant leap in sales of their boards, but it was also made to help promote the sport of skateboarding in general—to get kids out on their boards again. It worked. The video sold more copies than Stacy could have ever imagined.

"We originally made them as a promotional item, but we sold, like, 30,000 copies," he told *Surfer* magazine. "Our distributors worldwide were telling us that we were lifting the tide of skateboarding because one kid would buy one and a hundred kids would see it."

The success of the *Bones Brigade Video Show* meant the skaters on the Powell Peralta team were no longer toiling away in obscurity. They were making decent salaries and were on the verge of becoming skateboarding stars. Skateboarding was on the rebound, and Tony Hawk and his teammates were competing and participating in skate demos all the time.

Nowadays, thanks to improvements in digital technology, skateboard companies churn out more videos than anyone could possibly have time to watch, but in the mid-1980s, putting together a video was still a monumental task. Two years elapsed before Stacy began work on the second Bones Brigade video, *Future Primitive*, but it was worth the wait. The video was an enormous success and perfectly showcased the enormous talent within the group.

After filming Tony's part for the video, Stacy told him, "You have the talent to win any contest you want from now on." Stacy was right, and by his senior year in high school, Tony was a bonafide skateboarding superstar.

The two first Bones Brigade videos were hugely successful, but the third video, *The Search for Animal Chin*, is the one that everyone remembers from the era. After the Bones Brigade summer tour of 1986, the team blocked off four months to film the movie. The movie had a goofy storyline: the skaters were traveling around the world looking for the original skateboarder, a mythical guy named Won Ton Animal Chin, who—according to legend—had been forced underground by dark forces at work in the skateboarding world. In the film, the Bones Brigade sets out to find Chin, traveling the world skating and having fun. The film has one basic message: skate, above all else, for fun—not for money or fame. There are scenes of the Brigaders skating everything from a long drainage ditch in Hawaii and the streets of Chinatown to a launch ramp in a park and an empty pool at a motel. There's even a scene of Rodney Mullen and Per Welinder freestyling on the dance floor at a cheesy party.

Skateboarding was once again becoming one of the most popular activities for young people, and the Bones Brigade members were riding high.

"It was just such a good time," Steve Caballero told Canadian skateboard magazine *Concrete Powder*. "The team was winning a bunch of contests, and we decided we just wanted to do this video that showed amazing skating and us traveling around the world."

The climax of *Animal Chin* occurs in the desert, where the Brigade builds a giant vert ramp with a spine in the middle of it (meaning it was basically two giant half-pipes stuck together end-to-end).

The skaters, Tommy Guerrero, Lance Mountain, Mike McGill, Steve Caballero and Tony Hawk, take turns skating the ramp and then come together for a no-holds-barred team session. The footage is legendary, like nothing that had been seen up until that point.

"The double, triple and quadruple runs were all spontaneous," Steve remembers. "We hadn't even seen the ramp prior to filming, so when we got there, we just started skating."

At the end of the session, the team removed a lower section of the spine, creating a tunnel linking the two ramps. They dropped in one ramp and shot through the tunnel to catch air on the far side of the other ramp. You can tell by watching the movie that the team was having a lot of fun skating it, even as they flew through the air almost 20 feet above the desert floor.

Even though he's mostly known for his contribution to the growing street-skating scene during the 1980s, Tommy held his own on the giant ramp, knocking out some inverted handplants (or inverts), frontside and backside airs and some long, styled out grinds.

For his part, Steve nailed huge airs over the channel (a part of the lip of the ramp cut out for rolling in) judo airs (where you kick your front foot off the board in the air) and giant transfers over the spine. Mike whipped out some huge backside airs, inverted handplants and, of course, his signature move, the McTwist. Lance pulled huge alley-oop airs (the skater's body turns in the opposite direction from which he is traveling across the ramp), crail slides (the tail of the board is slid across the coping while the skater grabs the nose of the board) and giant handplant transfers over the channel.

Tony reached into his bag of tricks and pulled out Madonnas (the skater grabs the board and takes his front foot off, kicking it out behind him before landing his tail on the coping and re-entering the ramp), huge board slides, gay twist judo airs over the channel, backside varials, a backside ollie to tail, airwalks (the skater walks in the air while grabbing his board) and even a 720 (the double spin trick he'd learned the previous summer in Sweden).

During the double, triple and quadruple runs, the skaters were getting crazy. They were doing backside airs over frontside airs; back-to-back double McTwists on the spine; even four skaters doing handplants on the spine at once, as seen in a famous picture from the session.

The action was spontaneous, chaotic and dangerous, and Tony ended up paying the price, colliding head-on with Steve during a quadruple run. Battered and bruised, Tony quit for a day, missing out on the final bit of shooting. When *Chin* came out in May 1987, it swept through the world of skateboarding like a raging California brush fire, elevating the Bones Brigade into superstardom.

Soon after *Animal Chin*, Tony quit competitive skating for a while. The pressure on him to win was too intense. His methodical "robotic" style was impossible to match, and when someone actually beat Tony, the crowd would go nuts. He was so good that people were beginning to resent him.

"If I did a trick no one else did but had done it in the past three contests, it didn't count as much and wasn't as impressive as the first time," he wrote in his autobiography. "If another skater did the same trick I did, he scored higher."

Tony was through with competing, so he took his winnings and his royalty checks, bought a house in Fallbrook, California, and proceeded to build a giant vert ramp connected to a wooden bowl and another smaller mini-ramp nearer the house. The set-up cost $30,000 and was featured in numerous ads and articles in *Transworld Skateboarding* and *Thrasher* during the late 1980s.

Tony eventually returned to competition in 1988, only months after "retiring," won a bunch of vert contests and put together a part for the fourth Bones Brigade video, *Public Domain*. The unstoppable machine was back at it, and his contribution to vert skating's progression would continue for more than a decade, culminating in the explosive moment every skate fan remembers at the 1999 X-Games. But we'll get to that.

Chapter Eleven

Vert's Troubled Prince

My all-time favorite. Style, power, control, everything a skateboarder wanted to be. One hundred percent skater for life.

–Jay Adams on Christian Hosoi

The Bones Brigade members weren't the only skateboarders laying waste to pools and ramps in the 1980s. Several other companies also fielded teams with insanely talented skaters. Neil Blender was blowing minds for G&S. Coming out of Texas was the powerful Jeff Phillips. Lester Kasai was ruling the airways for Sims. But the main challenge to the dominant force of the Bones Brigade came from Christian Hosoi and Mark "Gator" Rogowski.

"With his finesse he made s**t look so easy that he had you thinking you could do the same, even though you never could," Christian Hosoi's friend Cesario Montano said of Christian's skating.

"With his fluidity, he made skateboarding look like his destiny."

"He was an exceptional phenomenon, charming, smoking pot constantly, attracting besotted females left and right and wearing atrocious ensembles of pink and white Jimmy Z clothes, shirts with the necks and sleeves cut off, silly headbands and numerous trinkets and bracelets. Occasionally he wore spandex or fishnet stockings," said Jocko Weyland.

Some people may have questioned Christian's sense of style, but there was no doubting his ability to ride a skateboard. According to Salba, he was, and is, simply the greatest skater that ever lived.

Vert skateboarding contests in the 1980s often came down to a battle for first place between Tony Hawk and Christian Hosoi. The two ramp rippers couldn't have been more different. Tony was a suburban white kid with a technical approach to skateboarding that matched his penchant for gadgetry. Christian was a Japanese-Hawaiian phenom whose skateboarding was less about tricks and more about huge airs drenched with enough style to justify his penchant for crazy outfits. Christian seemed to spend enough time in the air over the ramp to do whatever he wanted.

Christian was born in L.A., but his parents were from Hawaii. They moved back to the islands when Christian was seven years old. Soon after moving back, he got his first skateboard. A family friend sent a pair of Cadillac wheels and Chicago trucks to Christian for his birthday, and Ivan, an avid surfer who made and repaired his own surfboards, made a skateboard for his son in the shape of a surfboard.

It was the early 1970s, and skateboard design was still in its infancy. The board Ivan made had an upturned nose and a downturned tail that Ivan had designed to be used as a brake. Christian soon switched the board around, using the upturned kicktail to pivot the board around and control his direction.

Shortly after Christian got his first board, the Hosoi family moved back to L.A., where Ivan built a small ramp for his son. Christian skated the ramp almost every day with his friend Aaron Murray. The first time he skated at a skatepark was in 1977 at Skateboard World in Torrance, California.

When Ivan and Christian's mother, Bonnie, separated a few years later, Ivan devoted himself to fostering Christian's emerging talent. "Every day we'd go to the parks. Big-O. Marina. Skateboard World," Ivan told Keith David Hamm during an interview for Hamm's book, *Scarred For Life*. "He was so into it. I'd just let him guide me."

Christian was living in a rough neighborhood in L.A., and street gangs were constantly harassing him on his way to school. His only salvation was through skateboarding, hanging out and skating the concrete parks around the city. Finally, the harassment at school was just too much to take, and his father pulled him out. Ivan then became the manager of Marina Del Ray skatepark. Christian could hardly believe his luck.

"I'm going, 'You're kidding, right? This is a dream come true.' Now I'm going there every single day. And I open up the place. Sweep out the bowls. All the pinball machines, video games that I wanted to play. The snack bar was mine. The pro shop was mine. I was in there just running the whole place. And everybody's like, man, you're gonna be good when you get older."

They couldn't have been more right. Christian was already good, and while he haunted Marina Del Ray, he just continued to get better. Acid-dropping (rolling off the edge with speed) into the gnarliest pools and airing way out over the lip without fear, he was consistently placing among the top skaters at contests, beating out guys who were twice his age.

Christian's first picture in a skateboard magazine, which appeared in a 1980 issue of *Skateboarder*, shows him launching a stylish ollie a few feet over the lip of one of Marina Del Ray's smaller bowls. A picture taken a year later shows Christian flying almost head high out of the skatepark's deep pool. He was 13 at the time. Looking at the two photos, the speed of Christian's progression is obvious. Christian got his first sponsor at age 10 and turned pro when he was 13. Soon he was making $1600 a month and establishing himself as one of the few big-name pros at the time.

In the early years, he was sponsored by Z-Flex, Powell and Dogtown, but Sims released Christian's first pro-model skateboard in 1982. The graphic was of the Japanese rising sun with Hosoi written in a Japanese font across it. Christian could never settle on a sponsor, and soon afterward he quit Sims to ride for Alva, where he released the first swallow-tail skateboard. He then quit Alva to start his own company, Hosoi skateboards. Christian designed a board called a "Hammerhead," with handles carved out of the edges just forward of the front wheels.

"I was looking for a hook for my hand," he told *Transworld Skateboarding*. "I said, 'Oh, this looks hot!' It's completely original. No one was experimenting with any type of shapes back then."

To keep things confusing, Hosoi had his original Hammerhead skateboard design manufactured by several different companies—Santa Cruz, Skull Skates and Madrid skateboards. It was also bootlegged, further adding to the confusion.

As time went on, Christian's fame just continued to grow. He weathered skating's slump in the early 1980s, adapting easily to the backyard ramp scene after most of the skateparks closed.

"Yeah, skateboarding kinda had a lull, to the public," he told Hamm. "But to the pros it was thriving. We were searching out spots, going to Europe, doing full tours over there."

Other skaters would show up for backyard ramp contests and just sit and watch in awe as Christian blasted way over their heads. He floated effortlessly and seemingly without fear before dropping down onto the ramp and pumping so hard for speed on the transitions that the whole structure would shake. His power was awesome to behold.

As skateboarding regained its feet, Hosoi became a bona fide superstar, making scads of money and drawing loads of attention wherever he went. The fact that he was also a nice guy didn't hurt his popularity either.

"Even after a contest was over and every other pro was gone, Christian would still be in the parking lot, spending time with the kids, giving them stickers, signing autographs, talking to them and being cool," former pro Dave Duncan told the editors of *Built to Grind*.

Throughout the 1980s, Christian continued to drive the sport with his unique style and approach. Spending so much time in the air allowed him to invent moves like the Christ Air, where he assumed the position of Christ on the cross, with his board in one hand and his arms and legs outstretched, before gathering it all back together and finessing his wheels down onto the transition.

As former pro skater Eddie Reategui explains in *Built to Grind*, Hosoi was the ultimate showman. Before his contest run, Reategui says, Christian would be, "dancing, adjusting his s**t, looking around and making sure his five shirts hanging off him were showing the right logos. Then, all of a sudden, he'd drop in and win the contest, just blow doors. The place would erupt."

When street skating came on the scene during the latter half of the 1980s, Christian said no problem. Adjusting his high-flying attack to the obstacles littering the course, he claimed numerous victories.

Wearing a pair of tie-dyed yellow surf shorts and a loose-fitting white tank top, Christian ruled the course at the first Savannah Slamma street-skating contest in Savannah, Georgia, in 1987. In the words of *Thrasher* editor Kevin Thatcher, Christian "ricocheted like a cannon ball throughout the battleground. His speed lines and command of the sword met no match on this day. His frontside wall rides were so long they ran out of wall."

Two years later, at the third Savannah Slamma, Christian once again dominated. "Hosoi ruled the course with mastery and momentum," wrote *Thrasher* contributor, Miles.

Christian ruled the 1980s, but when skating changed direction during the early 1990s, and hero worshipping was replaced by a cynical culture revolving around technical trickery and a defiant urge to break with skating's past, Christian was left out in the cold. The skateboard superstar who had been earning upward of $300,000 a year was in trouble. The upstart companies he had a hand in were floundering, and his high-flying lifestyle was taking its toll. Christian got into drugs, namely crystal methamphetamine, and soon he couldn't skate without getting high. His skating suffered, and eventually he pretty much stopped skating all together, at least in public. "With Christian and his ego, there's no way he'd skate if he was going to skate bad," Eddie Reategui told Hamm.

Christian put off dealing with his drug problem for years, until one day he got busted trying to bring a large amount of crystal meth from California to Hawaii. He spent four years in a federal prison before being released on June 4, 2004. While incarcerated, Christian was able to clean up his drug habit, earn his high school diploma, get married and study the Bible to the point where he became a certified, card-carrying, born-again Christian. Christ had found God.

The day after he was released, Christian showed up at the A'ala Park skate shop in Honolulu, set up a board and headed over to the Kamiloiki skatepark to blow minds. Despite being off his board for so many years, Christian killed the park, ripping long, laid-back slides, backside airs and frontside grinds.

Less than two weeks later, pictures went public showing Christian destroying the Hanger Bowl in Honolulu, even pulling one of his signature Christ Airs. Make no mistake, it's the second coming.

Chapter Twelve

Gator: Fall from Grace

Mark Rogowski was the definition of the word "ripper."
—Jake Phelps (Thrasher Editor)

For Mark Anthony Rogowski, it's too late for a second chance. Gator—as the other 1980s vert hero was known to his fans—blew it all away one night in March 1991, when the dark side of his personality drove him to rape and kill his ex-girlfriend's best friend. Although Gator covered up his tracks at first, guilt eventually got the better of him, and he turned himself in to the authorities. He's now serving a life sentence for the rape and murder of aspiring model Jessica Bergsten. Rogowski is eligible for parole in 2010.

Despite the horrible mark on his reputation as a human being, no one can argue with Gator's contribution to skateboarding in the 1980s. By the time he was 16, Gator was a pro skateboarder making upward of $100,000 a year. "I was young, rich and popular," he wrote in an open letter to the skateboarding community printed in a 1996 issue of *Thrasher*. "My life was full of limousines, nice homes, new cars, world travel, concerts and going around with actors, models and rock stars."

With his high-flying antics and outspoken personality, Gator had a lot of crossover appeal, and he appeared regularly on television, on the radio and in magazines around the world to promote his sport.

Gator was born in Brooklyn, New York, but he moved to California, just outside of San Diego, with his mother and brother when he was three, just after his parents got divorced. When he was seven, Gator discovered skateboarding, and by the age of 10 he was a full-fledged skateboarder, haunting the local parks around his suburban home in Escondido.

Coming from a cash-strapped home, Gator didn't fit in with the rest of his suburban skateboarder friends, who were also into surfing and buying the latest fashions. He started hanging out full-time at the skateparks, rolling with a tougher crowd of die-hard skaters.

"These guys were so into it, having such a good time, sweatin' and laughin' and crackin' jokes, and just snakin' each other," he told *Thrasher*. "It was a full soul session, everybody just shreddin' it up." Gator's talent grew, and soon he was picking up sponsors and winning contests. By age 14, as a sponsored amateur riding for G&S skateboards and Vans shoes, Gator was on his way to becoming a poster child for the 1980s vert revolution.

Tony Hawk's father started the National Skateboarding Association in 1983 to help bring some credibility to the sport that had grabbed his son's attention. The NSA, as it was known, held a contest, the Del Mar Spring Nationals, at the Del Mar skatepark in the spring of 1984. Tony was ruling, but Gator stole the show, winning the contest and grabbing the attention of up-and-coming skateboard manufacturer Brad Dorfman. That day, after the contest, Dorfman signed Gator to his new company, Vision.

When Vision issued Gator's signature vortex board, it became one of the bestselling boards of all time, earning him up to $14,000 a month in royalties. With his good looks, tremendous skills on a skateboard and unlimited knack for self-promotion, Gator was soon on a roll, on his way to the top of the world.

It all had to do with his attitude. Gator was hungry for attention, so hungry that even after he was finished skateboarding for the day he had to be front and center. His partying antics were legendary. He'd often get naked just to freak people out, and once he even skated a pool naked for a Vision ad. In 1986, Gator got arrested at a ramp contest in

Virginia when he punched a police officer. After Dorfman bailed him out, he returned to the contest and placed sixth. Of course, the skateboarding community ate it up. Gator was the bad boy with the talent to back up the attitude.

"Gator was the rebel of the group," wrote Jesse Pearson in an article in *Vice*, a popular youth culture magazine. "He was the one who burned fastest and to whom image was most important. His concern with appearances had its negative effects on the sport for sure (crass commercialism, style over substance), but it also benefited skating hugely by upping its public image. This era, more than any other, birthed the mythos of skating as a countercultural, punk rock, cool thing that you should start doing during the years when you hate your parents."

Gator wanted to be skateboarding's ambassador. He was determined to turn the whole world onto the sport that had brought him fame and fortune. But in spite of his outspokenness, he was respected among his fellow skaters, mainly because he possessed an insane level of skill. When McGill introduced the McTwist, for example, Gator was one of the first skaters to learn it. He even had a move named after him—the Gatair, a 360 air with a grab.

One kid who idolized Gator was future skateboarding superstar Danny Way, whom Gator helped get on the Vision team.

"I grew up skating at Del Mar Skate Ranch watching guys like Gator," Danny told *Thrasher* in a 2003 interview. "I'd see Hosoi there occasionally, but watching Gator, I'd say they're kind of on the same level in a lot of ways. Gator's line selection was incredible. He'd get speed out of things and you're like, where are you coming from with it? People didn't realize—maybe people did, but I think Gator was ahead of his time."

Near the end of the 1980s, Gator made a move that was very unpopular with his skateboarding peers: he changed his name, substituting his estranged father's name, Rogowski, for his own more media-friendly middle name, Anthony. Now, he'd gone too far, putting himself in the same league as pop stars like Prince and Madonna.

Gator crisscrossed the U.S. and traveled all over the world, skating demos and competitions, most notably as the banner name for the Swatch Impact Tour, a high-flying, big-money BMX, skateboarding and roller skating demo.

One day, his vert-riding buddy Christian Hosoi introduced him to Brandi McClain, a beautiful 15-year-old from Arizona. McClain's friend Jessica Bergsten was seeing Christian at the same time. Brandi eventually left Arizona to live with Gator in California.

"Gator and Brandi were inseparable," wrote Cory Johnson in his article for the *The Village Voice*.

"They caroused all-night Carlsbad bars, made the scene at the San Diego parties. They were the hottest couple on the beach." Gator paid for everything. He bought Brandi plane tickets so she could come on the road with him, brand new cars and all the partying vices he could afford.

Around this time, things got away from Gator. His brash, self-centered personality was wearing on his relationship with Brandi. He was forever breaking it off with her and then getting back together. As well, just as it seemed his luck in skateboarding could never run out, the bottom fell out of vert skating's popularity. Skateboarders such as Gator, Tony Hawk and Steve Caballero had to adapt to the culture's massive change in direction, which favored street skateboarding.

Some skaters, like the aforementioned Bones Brigaders, were able to ride into street's rising wave, but for Gator, whose vert skating relied mainly on power and flow, it was over. With his ego, it was impossible to start at the bottom and to watch from the sidelines as thousands of young nobodies rolled across parking lots effortlessly flipping their boards. Gator's popularity disintegrated almost overnight. Skating's new street army wanted nothing more than to distance their sport from its association with the vert-riding, Day-Glo dinosaurs of the 1980s.

"People put you on a pedestal. Gator was an idol," Jason Jessee told Helen Stickler, the filmmaker behind *Stoked: the Rise and Fall of Gator,* a documentary released in 2003. "Then, you're not that big of a deal anymore. Disposable hero. It's just, see ya later."

Gator was in West Germany for a contest in 1989, by which time his pro career was in its dying stages. He spent the night after the contest getting totally wasted, wandering from party to party, fighting with a bartender and a cab driver. At the end of the night, he almost ended up killing himself when he fell trying to climb into the window of his hotel.

Gator's fall was broken by a wrought-iron fence, which went through his neck, face and thumb. He survived, but with the knowledge that he had to make some serious changes in his life. Gator decided to get some help, and he sought out a friend in former surfer Augie Constantino, a born-again Christian who had found God after a similar drunken accident.

"I introduced Mark to a personal God," Constantino told Johnson for his article. "Mark never had a father to speak of. I showed Christ to him, and as the Bible says, He's our own true father. So of course that appealed to Mark."

Gator may have found God, but demons still lurked inside of him. Almost overnight, he became a fanatical preacher, lecturing his skateboard buddies between runs, and worst of all, alienating the girl he loved by condemning her licentiousness and telling her they were forbidden to have sex until they were married.

Brandi, having grown used to a lifestyle that revolved around as much sex, drugs and partying as she could ever want, refused to go along with her boyfriend's plans for a devout Christian life. She left him, and he freaked. Then, when he found out she was dating someone else, he threatened to kill her. Brandi decided to run away to New York, not telling anyone except her family where she was going.

When Brandi's friend Jessica showed up in San Diego a few weeks later, she was looking for a party. Not knowing what had happened between her friend and Gator, Jessica contacted him, and he agreed to meet her for lunch. Afterward, the two went back to Gator's home, ostensibly to hang out. Later, drunk and totally out of his mind with rage, Gator raped and strangled Jessica. He dumped her body in a shallow grave in the desert and went on with his life until finally confessing to the crime almost two months later.

"On that fateful evening, I lost all control of my anger and pain," Gator wrote in *Thrasher*. "It suddenly came out on a person I had been friends with for years. I realized afterward I was definitely not well."

Unfortunately, it was all a bit too late for Jessica. No amount of realization or remorse on Gator's part was going to bring her back.

The skateboarding world was more than happy to welcome Christian Hosoi back into the fold after his incarceration, realizing that his crime was a lapse in judgment stemming from his addiction to drugs. For Gator, if he ever gets out, it will be a different story. The horrific nature of his crime means that the Gator that the skateboard world knew and loved during the 1980s is effectively dead, replaced by a human being most people, save maybe his closest friends and family, would rather have nothing to do with.

"I hate prison, this life here and what I did back then," he wrote. "I may never get out. But unlike a bad dream, I can't just wake up out of it and go skateboarding. No fun, no freedom, no second chance."

Chapter Thirteen

The Rise of Street

In 1981, in the first issue of *Thrasher*, the editors implored skaters to remember their sport's roots and take skating back into the streets.

"A curb is an obstacle until you grind it," they wrote. "A wall is but a ledge until you drop off it. A cement bank is a useless slab of concrete until you shred it."

Everything is skateable, *Thrasher* told its readers. Forget about skateparks, ramps and empty pools for a second, and think about the ledge out front of your apartment building or the stairs down the street in front of the courthouse.

By the mid 1980s, street skating was taking over, initially out of necessity—people wanted to skate and there wasn't a ramp in every backyard—but eventually because that was what every kid wanted to do. Once skaters started realizing all the fun they could have grinding a curb at the 7-Eleven or ollieing off some stairs, skateboarding changed direction. Now there was something every kid could enjoy doing, no matter where they lived. As long as there was a spot of pavement within rolling distance of their house, they could head out the front door to practice their ollies or kickflips.

A few pioneers were responsible for popularizing street skateboarding in the early 1980s. One of the first was Bones Brigader Tommy Guerrero. From the day Tommy Guerrero borrowed his older brother Tony's skateboard, broke it and almost suffered a severe beating for his efforts, the San Francisco–born youngster was hooked. Early on, freestyle was his thing, but he could also be found ripping the cement parks ringing his hometown during the late 1970s.

Tommy's early effort to get on a skateboard team failed when the team decided to go with his older brother, Tony. Then, when skateboarding fizzled, just as the California punk scene was finding its feet, music became more important to Tommy than skateboarding. He played in a bunch of bands, including one with his brother called Free Beer. Tommy was rocking out in San Francisco's biggest punk clubs when he was still a minor.

Skateboarding was barely hanging on when *Thrasher* magazine came out, promoting a new, punker skateboarding image and encouraging skaters like Tommy to take their skating to the streets now that most of the parks had closed and skaters were once again a fringe element.

"When the parks closed, we had nowhere to go, so we skated whatever we could find," Tommy told the editors of *Built To Grind*." If there was a pool down the block, you skated the pool. If there was a full-pipe at the beach, you skated the full-pipe. If there was a jump ramp in the middle of a schoolyard, you skated that. It was never a conscious decision; we just skated."

Tommy grew up poor. Raised by his mother, he was constantly skipping school to hang out with his friends and go skating. "I just could not deal with school, could not deal with the teachers, the students, the system," he said during an interview with the *San Francisco Bay Guardian*. "I started cutting school. I'd go skating all day, every day. My mom was at work all day. She didn't know what was going on."

All Tommy's "hard work" eventually paid off, and he exploded onto the professional skateboard scene in the summer of 1983 at the first-ever street-style contest in San Francisco's Golden Gate Park. The set-up was little more than few banked ramps and the road, but Tommy took all he'd learned in the previous years of taking ramp tricks and freestyle into the streets of San Francisco and laid waste to the assembled course. He was an amateur at the time, but that didn't stop him from winning the pro category.

In the words of Jocko Weyland, it was, "a symbolic victory on par with the Z-Boys emergence at the Del Mar Nationals 10 years before." Street skating was so novel at the time that barely anyone was even doing flatland ollies. Rodney Mullen had only figured out how to do it about a year before the contest. But by the time the contest went down, as Jocko points out in his book *Scarred for Life*, "Tommy was already consistently ripping down the streets of San Francisco, ollieing over shrubs, doing 15-foot curb grinds—and whatever else came into his mind—with a nonchalance that made it look easy."

The following year, Tommy signed with Stacy Peralta and joined the Bones Brigade as the first-ever pro street shredder. Stacy realized that if his team was going to stay on top of skateboarding in the 1980s, they were going to have to hold it down on the streets as well. When Tommy's part in Stacy's second film, *Future Primitive*, dropped, the skateboarding world was turned on its head. Skating was fun again, and you could do it anywhere.

Tommy flew around the world with the Bones Brigade, skating for adoring fans all over. The high school dropout from San Francisco was earning $70,000 a year by the time he was 17. It seemed ditching school to skate had paid off. Tommy skated as a pro for years, eventually leaving Powell to start his own company, Real, with fellow street skater Jim Thibeaud.

Another pioneer of street skating in the 1980s was Mark Gonzales, a young high school dropout from Los Angeles, who's still considered one of the most creative skateboarders who ever lived.

"Probably nothing, and almost definitely nobody, better represents what it is to skateboard than Mark Gonzales," wrote *Slap* skateboard magazine editor Mark Whiteley.

"He's quite simply the most revered and worshipped dude to ever step on a stunt wood. It's not the list of tricks he's done, but how he did them," added *Thrasher* writer Scott Dawdler.

Mark's laid-back style and insane moves meant that when he was skating, others simply watched. Throughout the '80s and right on through the '90s, Gonz, as he's known by skaters worldwide, was busy laying waste to the urban environment and drawing attention to the fact that rad skating could happen anywhere, even on the curb in front of your own house.

Like Tommy Guerrero, Mark was ripping from an early age, picking up a sponsorship from Tony Alva's company when he was still in his early teens. By the time Gonz turned 16 years old, he was ready to go pro for Brad Dorfman's Vision Skateboards. His talent was obvious to anyone who saw him skate.

Gonz was always ahead of his time. When *Thrasher* put on the first Savannah Slamma street skating contest in 1987, Gonz was already experimenting with switch-stance skateboarding, something that wouldn't become popular until well into the next decade. At that same contest, he pulled huge frontside boardslides down the makeshift rail on the street course. A frontside boardslide (where the skater slides his board while facing backward on the rail) is one of the most stylish tricks in skateboarding and is still considered tough almost 20 years later. During his final run at the same contest, Gonz also moved a jump ramp in front of the rail, launched off it and slid his board *up* the rail onto the platform. He was famous for such innovations. He always had to take a different approach to skateboarding.

In 1982, Rodney Mullen took Alan Gelfand's revolutionary ollie to the flatground, snapping his tail on the ground and lifting his board into the air by dragging his front foot up the length of the board. Around the time Tommy Guerrero won the first street-style contest in San Francisco's Golden Gate Park, the ollie was finding its way into the street, and Gonz was one of the first to master its application to the urban environment.

In *Scarred for Life*, Jocko Weyland describes seeing Gonz ollie at an early Huntingdon Beach street contest. "A feral kid riding a pink Alva Fishtail skated exceedingly well and won sponsored amateur, doing ollies in a way that I had never seen before, effortlessly soaring by popping the tail of his board. That was Mark Gonzales."

Later, Weyland describes the scene at a street contest in Oregon in 1986. "Insanity ensued in the rain as Mark did a rock-and-roll boardslide on a vintage Cadillac's fin and landed it. It was an epoch-defining moment."

That same year, Gonz launched the gap-ollieing craze, still popular among skateboarders today, when he blasted a huge ollie at San Francisco's most popular skate spot, Embarcadero. He decided to jump from the top of one of the architectural features that was designed like a wave, over a huge flat spot where he had been landing earlier, to land farther away on a large stage. The enormous gap was christened the Gonz gap and became the distance by which all other gaps were measured for the next decade.

Gonz was an accomplished vert skater as well, and like his street-skating counterpart Tommy Guerrero, he brought vert tricks into the streets, doing handplants and bonelesses (a move where you grab your board, step one foot off and launch yourself into the air) everywhere and anywhere. Mark Gonzales and his street skateboarding pal Natas Kaupas also began trying to take Rodney Mullen's ollie flip innovations into the street.

It's hard to place an exact time and date on when the Gonz became a skateboarding legend, but his reputation grew throughout the 1980s, culminating in his revolutionary part in Blind Skateboard's 1991 film, *Video Days*. Even though Blind (the company Gonz started with Steve Rocco after leaving Vision) released the film at a time when skateboarding was once again experiencing a major downturn in popularity, *Video Days* became one of the most legendary skate videos of all time. With Gonz' incredible part as its anchor, it's not hard to see why. Even by today's standards, the part is insane.

The section opens with Gonz effortlessly flowing down a street, tic-tacking (lifting the front of his board and turning it from side to side, creating a forward momentum) and carving his board from side to side. It looks like a scene from a 1970s skateboarding movie—until Gonz pops a frontside 180 ollie and heads backward toward a short flight of stairs. No problem, you're thinking to yourself, until he half-cabs (a 180 ollie from backward to forward) into a grind going down the ledge beside the stairs. Suddenly, the skateboarding you're seeing is totally new and outrageous, except, you have to remember, it happened over 15 years ago!

In the next sequence, as some smooth John Coltrane jazz plays in the background, Gonz sets up with a high frontside shuv-it (an ollie where your board spins 180 degrees underneath your feet) down three stairs. Rolling with his circa-1991 directional skateboard backward under his feet,

Gonz then ollies a frontside 180 off the nose into a backward 50-50 grind (a double-truck grind) down a handrail. Time has ceased to make sense. Is this for real? Was this really caught on film over 15 years ago? Gonz's skating is so smooth, so innovative, so technical, that it defies time.

A backside 360 ollie pivot on the flat, followed by a frontside 360 ollie off a small drop onto the sidewalk, nollies to nose manuals (ollieing off the nose of the board up onto a curb, then riding while balancing on the front wheels), an ollie grab down a giant set of stairs called the Wallenberg Big Four (which is still a challenge for top skaters to this day), a huge boardslide down a kinked rail that very few skaters would try to slide, a nose blunt slide (a slide on the nose of the board, with the board pointing straight down toward the ground), a kickflip boardslide, a boardslide to frontside shuv-it on a complicated zig-zag rail—the litany of tricks Gonz pulls during his part in *Video Days* is the stuff of legend.

Interviews with Gonz reveal little about the man. His answers to questions are cryptic at best. One thing's for sure, Gonz is a different type of skater, a multi-dimensional artist of the streets. Over the last decade, his talent has branched out into different areas—namely poetry, fiction, art and the business of selling skateboards. He's gone from doodling on his griptape with a magic marker to staging one-man multimedia shows, and his art has appeared in galleries all around the world. Gonz is still active in skateboarding, running his company Krooked and causing a stir wherever he goes.

Shortly after Gonz hit the scene, another skater by the name of Natas Kaupas was also hard at work reinventing the process of rolling down the street on a skateboard. By 1986, Natas was sponsored by Skip Engblom's company, Santa Monica Airlines, and his unique approach to street skating had earned him a place alongside Tommy Guerrero and Mark Gonzales.

Natas' two parts in the Santa Cruz skateboard films *Wheels of Fire* and *Streets on Fire*, which came out in 1988 and 1989 respectively, provided a major leg-up to street skating worldwide. In the first of the two films, Natas ollies over a garbage can on the flat. At that time, nobody could ollie nearly as high as the big guy with the easy-going grin and trademark shock of bleach-blond hair.

"This is me, going down the street," Natas tells viewers by way of a cheesy voice-over during *Wheels of Fire*. "Oh, how's it going? Hi Dad. Just doin' a little skating," he deadpans as the camera rolls past a bum sitting on a bench smoking a cigarette.

Natas then proceeds to effortlessly work his way through an endless list of street tricks—one-footed ollie 180s, wheelies (known to skaters as manuals), curb grinds, ollie airwalks, wall rides—Natas showed kids that skating was fun. Go on, give it a try, his attitude said. It doesn't matter if you look like a dork—keep skating, learn more tricks, make jokes, hang out with your friends. Forget about those guys flying high up in the air over vert ramps you'll never ride—this is what it's all about. *This* is skateboarding.

Before long, Natas began hopping onto rails, like Gonz, trying boardslides and grinds and taking skateboarding in a whole new direction. According to *Transworld Skateboarding* contributor Mackenzie Eisenhour, both Gonz and Natas slid their boards down the same 10-stair rail at the Westwood Federal Building in Los Angeles on the same day in 1986. It was a whole new thing. Suddenly street skating was daring, dangerous and just as exciting as any vert session. Hit the rail and prove to your friends you were committed to skating, even if it meant nutting yourself on a bar a few times before landing the slide.

The next year, in *Streets on Fire,* Natas blew the skateboarding world away. Skating to fIREHOSE's song "Brave Captain," Natas roars into the frame, tailsliding a curb for about 10 feet. In the next sequence, he ollies onto a fire hydrant, spinning around on the top of it twice before dismounting. It's an amazing feat of balance and dexterity.

For the next five minutes, Natas unloads a bag full of tricks three times the size of what he'd brought to the table the year before in *Wheels of*

Fire. When you compare both parts, you get an idea of the speed of street skating's progression around this time. Natas lipslides a long flat rail and boardslides the same tall rail that he and Gonz slid years earlier, this time landing backward (or fakie).

For his last trick, Natas ollies off a small launch ramp and boardslides the roll bars of a jeep, dropping to the ground about four feet on the other side of the vehicle. You can just imagine what effect this trick had on the Bones Brigade generation. Now, it seemed anything was possible. The tools for getting radical were everywhere.

Natas was famous for having the first signature skateboard shoe, released by Etnies in 1987. Natas was also famous for having a name that when spelled backward was Satan. In the outsider-dominated culture of skateboarding, this didn't hurt his board sales. Finally, Natas will always be remembered for having the most controversial skateboard graphic ever. In 1991, he started his own board company, 101, with the help of freestyle-turned-industry-mogul Steve Rocco. Natas' pro model for 101 sported a picture of a dead pope on a rope, a decapitated baby, an inverted pentagram and the devil himself. On top of this, the graphic was printed upside down to further freak out the suspicious masses. Shortly afterward, Natas quit the skateboarding scene, but his influence and impact—as well as his last pro board—will forever be remembered.

Chapter Fourteen

Industry OVERhaul

I like the name World Industries. It sounds so... cosmopolitan.

–Jake Phelps. *Thrasher.* 1990.

Skateboarding never died. The only thing dead was the manufacturers who couldn't adapt to a changing environment, an environment they considered hostile because they couldn't understand it. But that environment was the very place where skateboarding was born and to which it is now returning. That environment is the streets.

–Steve Rocco, April 1986

By the time Mark Gonzales' famous video part in Blind's *Video Days* came out in 1991, the skateboarding industry had changed drastically, largely thanks to one man, Steve Rocco. Steve Rocco's World Industries skateboard company would come to define the sport's direction at the end of the 1980s and well into the 1990s. Unlike his counterparts at skateboarding giants Vision, Powell and Peralta and Santa Cruz, Rocco realized that skating's new breed was looking for something less corporate. Skaters didn't want to be sold to by a bunch of working stiffs. They wanted products that represented what skateboarding was all about to them, something underground and anti-establishment. Rocco's guerrilla approach of making only as many boards as he could afford and marketing them directly to skateboarding's new breed of disenchanted street urchins worked wonders, and World Industries took off while the larger companies that had defined skating in the 1980s failed.

In the 1980s, Steve Rocco was an elite freestyle skater, looked up to by all, including Rodney Mullen, for his innovations and offbeat style. In 1987, Rocco was kicked off the Sims team for getting out of line one too many times. Seeing little future in his own professional career, Rocco decided to start a skateboarding company. With a little help from skateboarding godfather Skip Engblom, who was running his company, Santa Monica Airlines, at the time, Steve launched Santa Monica Airlines: Rocco Division.

At first, Steve's company only sponsored three pros: Jeff Hartsell, Jesse Martinez and himself. Thankfully, his best friend Rodney Mullen, who was still riding for Powell, agreed to help out with the company. Besides lending money to Steve to help with the start-up costs, Rodney also moved out to California to live with his friend and help with the day-to-day operations of the company. Obviously, when George Powell found out that Rodney and Steve were working together on launching a new company, he wasn't too happy about it.

Understanding Rodney's friendship with Steve, George offered to buy out Rodney's investment in Steve's company if Rodney would stay with Powell. The bond of friendship between Steve and Rodney was too strong, though, and Rodney decided to throw in his lot with his freestyle friend. Rodney could see where skateboarding was going, and he trusted in Steve's ability to adapt to the changing landscape.

"His ear was to the ground, and he knew that skating was dying," Rodney wrote in his autobiography. "The industry was in a slump, board sales were dropping at an alarming rate, fewer people were becoming interested in skating, and the ones who were interested wanted rawer companies with more street credentials."

Freestyling was as good as dead at this point, and Rodney knew his own best chances for survival lay in working for Steve behind the scenes. "Steve was the only friend I had ever had, and if our ship was going to sink I wanted to be on it with him."

It took a while, but Steve and Rodney's ship eventually sailed, and it kept on sailing through skateboarding's third and final industry-wide slump during the early 1990s, eventually making both Steve and Rodney millionaires when they took their company public.

Santa Monica Airlines: Rocco Division became World Industries after Santa Cruz, the company that owned the Santa Monica Airlines name, got upset when Steve ran an ad for his Gizmo wheels, cynically outlining the process behind the manufacturing of skateboard wheels. At the end of his diatribe against the skateboard wheel industry, Steve made what would be a typically direct entreaty to skateboarders—buy his products or don't.

"Try out some Gizmos. If you like them, keep them. If you don't, sell them to some of your friends and go try something else, because the only true test of a good wheel is if it works well for you."

In essence, Steve was saying, "It matters about as much to me as it does to you if I survive this round of the skateboard game." Of course, the kids loved it, and World Industries soon became the most successful company in the marketplace. At the time, Steve and Rodney's company was so small, though, that they could hardly meet the demand for their boards. Ironically, the difficulty in acquiring World Industries product only increased demand.

Word spread among pro skaters that World Industries was doing things differently. World's bosses were skaters. They didn't care what their team members did off their boards, what they wore, or how they acted. They were constantly changing their board graphics, and they were playing fast and loose with the established rules of the skateboarding industry. They displayed the kind of rebelliousness that skaters have identified with ever since the Dogtown days.

One skater who took notice was Powell's rising street star, Mike Vallely. "Vallely was huge, the biggest new star in skateboarding, and any team would have killed to have him ride for them," Rodney wrote in *The Mutt*. Rodney and Steve knew that if Mike joined them at World Industries, their company would explode.

Mike, an outsider by nature, didn't like all the rules governing skaters who rode for Powell. He wanted out, and he told Rodney. The two quit Powell at the same time, and suddenly World was huge. Mike V's board for World Industries was a double kick board, much like the ones used by virtually every skateboarder today. The board was revolutionary in more ways than one, as skateboard writer and collector Sean Cliver explained in an article he wrote for *Transworld Skateboarding*.

"Not only does this board have the distinction of being the harbinger of modern street skating and deck shapes, but the Barnyard graphic was the first to truly break the punk mold of the '80s with full nose-to-tail cartoon art and Day-Glo fluorescent colors," he explained.

The boards flew off the shelves, becoming the big seller for World Industries and pushing their earnings through the roof. World Industries was defining the times. "The other huge companies could never connect in the dirtball, ghetto way we did," wrote Rodney. Knowing this, the other companies tried to sink World Industries by joining forces against them, but it was no use—they were just too strong.

Mark Gonzales loved the way things worked at World Industries. "He was pretty amazed that we did whatever we wanted, and he wanted to be a part of it," wrote Steve Rocco in a short history of his company.

In 1990, Gonz told Rocco he wanted to start his own company called Blind, the opposite of his current sponsor, Vision. Steve agreed to help him start the company, and Blind was born, the first of many spin-off companies that would operate out of the World Industries warehouse. Later, Natas

Kaupas also joined the World Industries machine and started his own company, 101 Skateboards.

Soon, World Industries had plucked away so many of the best skaters of the time that they had a stranglehold on the skateboard marketplace. One young skater who rode for World Industries and then joined Gonz at Blind was a young street ripper named Jason Lee. Jason was a phenom, considered the best pro riding for World Industries at the time. Originally, Steve was reluctant to let Jason leave World to ride for Blind, but in the end Steve realized it didn't really matter, since he stood to benefit from Blind's success as well.

Later, young, talented street rippers Guy Mariano and Rudy Johnson also joined Blind, and the company's popularity shot through the roof. They released *Video Days* in 1991, the video that set the standard for all videos to follow.

Chapter Fifteen

Skateboarding's New Breed

By the time *Video Days* came out, freestyle skateboarding was pretty much dead. However, many of the technical elements of freestyle were being borrowed by street skaters like Jason Lee. Lee took tricks like 360-degree kickflips (where the board spins 360 degrees while flipping one full revolution) from the freestyle arena into the street. Soon, such technical board control became about as important to street skaters as getting air had been to vert skaters. In essence, if you couldn't flip your board every which way and land on it like it was nothing, you were nothing.

Rodney Mullen recognized that the brand of skateboarding he had dominated for a decade had run its course, but he was reluctant to jump on the technical-street-skating bandwagon. He didn't think he had it in him to start all over again, to make his own inroads into street skating. Of course, everyone else knew he had it in him. One guy by the name of Mike Ternasky knew that if he could get Rodney to refocus his amazing skating abilities on the street, the king of freestyle could once again push the sport to the next level.

Mike Ternasky ran one of skateboarding's biggest new companies in the late 1980s, H-Street, with partner Tony Magnusson. When Tony and Mike released the first H-Street video in 1988, *Shackle Me Not*, it took the skateboarding world by storm, introducing everyone to up-and-coming phenoms like Ron Allan, Danny Way and the inimitable Matt Hensley. Hensley's domination of the street environment set him apart. It seemed to everybody watching that he could literally do anything he wanted on his skateboard—flipping it this way and that, sliding everything in sight and ollieing over huge stuff like benches and off ramps. Hensley ruled. H-Street ruled. Their next video, *Hocus-Pocus*, was even more successful, bringing loads of unknown skaters into the limelight, but somewhere along the line, there was a disagreement, and the Mike Ternasky–Tony Magnusson partnership dissolved.

In 1992, with Steve Rocco's help, Mike Ternasky started a new company called Plan B. He signed a bunch of the best street skaters of the time—Sean Sheffey, Mike Carroll, Rick Howard, Danny Way, Canadian phenom Colin McKay and Rodney—and set out to make the best skateboarding video yet.

While Plan B's other skaters were already busy filming for their parts, Mike persuaded Rodney to start riding a bigger board and adapting his tricks to the street. Rodney finally agreed.

When Plan B's video *Questionable* dropped in 1992, it provided a huge boost to skateboarding. It showcased so many tricks that kids everywhere literally ran out in the streets in a desperate effort to catch up to where their favorite pros and some unknown top-ranked amateurs had already gone.

In an interview for *Transworld Skateboarding*, pro Kyle Leeper remembers the effect *Questionable* had on him and his skate buddies.

"I borrowed *Questionable* from my friend at school," he remembers. "He told me I had to see it. He was this kid I looked up to because he was down and knew everything about skating. So I borrowed a copy on an 8mm tape and took it home to watch. I put on [Matt] Hensley's part, the intro, montage and [Pat] Duffy's part came on, and me and my homey Nick were tripping like, 'What is this?' We had no idea this was possible. We were laughing at it, totally blown away. And then my dad told me, 'Come on, it's time to go to baseball practice,' but I couldn't leave the TV. I was totally hooked. I went to practice and all I could think about was that video. Plan B's *Questionable* changed my life—from then on, skateboarding was all I ever wanted to do."

Although Hensley was already an established skateboard star, Pat Duffy was a complete unknown at the time. He literally exploded onto the scene with a video part that had no match. The part begins with Duffy's skater friend Joel Rona trying to boardslide a high, long handrail. After several attempts and several heavy falls, Joel is destroyed, his knee bleeding from a gaping wound. His friend Pat watches from a distance as Joel peels himself off the ground once again. Joel then turns to the camera. "You see, Pat. Pat is actually a Terminator," he says, pointing at the lens to emphasize his point. "He was supposed to kill someone, and he came from the future. But then his program malfunctioned. And so now he's invincible. He can fall on his face and it won't hurt him."

Then the music starts up—a manic song called *Tommy the Cat* by the genre-bending, early '90s supergroup Primus. The camera cuts to Pat roaring toward the same handrail that had just messed with his friend. Pat easily ollies his back wheels over the rail for a lipslide. Then, in the next shot, he ollies from the other side into a backside 50-50 grind. Then he frontside smith grinds the rail (a back truck grind where the front truck is poked at an angle off the side of the rail). Finally, he backside smith grinds it (same thing on the other, harder side). You can almost hear the gasps of disbelief echoing from over a decade ago. This stuff, particularly the backside smith grind, is gnarly even by today's standards.

The part doesn't end there, though. Duffy goes on to switch 360 ollie down some stairs, nose bluntslide some benches, backside smith grind a *kinked* rail and frontside 50-50 grind the longest rail anybody had ever attempted (to the shock and amazement of everyone in attendance, as can be heard from the screaming and shouting that follows). He also steps to a 50-50 grind down a huge, long, double-kinked round rail that defied what most people thought was possible to stay on at that time.

At the end of his part, Pat hops up into a backside lipslide (the skater approaches the rail with his back toward it, jumps his back wheels over the rail, lands in a twisted position and slides down with his heels facing the landing) on a monster rail *in the rain*! A backside lipslide on a huge wet, metal rail with a wet board and wet shoes was more insane than most people could even understand. Duffy did it, and he made it look easy.

"Duffy is definitely one of the building blocks of modern street skating," says Duffy's Plan B teammate Danny Way, during a voice-over for a recently released retrospective of the Plan B videos. "He created a whole movement. His overall skateboarding ability is so well-rounded."

Mike Ternasky had assembled the team, and because of the success of the H-Street video, he knew he wanted to make a video that would change everything in skateboarding. Forever.

He managed this with *Questionable*. It's not just Duffy either. The rest of the video also measures up—and then some.

Colin McKay and Danny Way were accomplished vert and street skaters by that time, and they were taking their difficult technical street tricks back onto the ramp, blowing the dust off vert skating and making it relevant once again. Danny's part opens with him knocking himself out by jumping off the roof of a house onto a trampoline. The film then cuts to him and a pre-pubescent Colin McKay beating the crap out of each other in Colin's parent's living room in Vancouver before showcasing the young maniacs destroying everything in their path on their skateboards. Danny and Colin typify the new skateboarder—someone equally at home ripping ramps, parks or anything in the street, including burly rails. There's nothing Danny and Colin can't skate, and it's scary, because Colin's voice hasn't even broken yet.

"We could have easily been like, 'Oh, let's just skate street,' but Danny and I liked vert so much," Colin said in an interview later in *Transworld Skateboarding*. "It was so fun to us that we stuck with trying to skate it, even though our friends skated street."

On the half-pipe, Danny pulls double kickflip indys, 540 tailgrabs, varial 540s, caballarial noseslides, heelflip indys and inward heelflips (I'm not even going to begin to try to explain what these tricks are). Then he takes it to the street, with backside lipslides down rails, a double kickflip down some stairs, some massively technical ledge trick combinations and one massive rail slide down the same giant double-kinked rail Duffy grinded in his part.

Looking like a slightly smaller version of Danny, with the same shaved head, huge pants, giant T-shirt and tiny skateboard wheels, Colin McKay tears apart the street spots and concrete parks of his native Vancouver during the opening to his part. He then lays waste to the indoor half-pipe at Canadian freestyle legend Mike Harris' indoor skatepark in nearby Richmond. McKay's part features some of the most technical ramp skating the world had yet seen. You have to feel sorry for the older guys standing on the deck of the ramp watching this little kid pull trick after impossible trick with what looks like next to no effort.

Mike Carroll, *Thrasher*'s Skater of the Year in 1994, turned in an incredible part for *Questionable*, too, ruling his local spot, the famed EMB ledges and stairs in San Francisco, with tricks and combinations nobody had ever seen.

Rodney Mullen's first-ever street-skating part comes at the end of the video, and it's nothing short of amazing. It's difficult to imagine how he had any doubt that he would be able to adapt his awesome skating abilities to the street. Listing off all the tricks he tosses out would take up the rest of this book. Now that there were so many new tricks to learn, how could skateboarding die out? Some may have doubted its ability to survive, but anyone who watched the first Plan B video knew that skaters had simply gone into hiding in a concerted effort to breathe new life into their favorite pastime.

A new day in skateboarding had dawned, and the gang at Plan B had been chosen to announce its arrival.

Many older skaters who had given up the sport during the leaner years also ran out to their local skateshops to buy one of the new, smaller, narrower double-kick boards that were equipped with an equally narrow pair of trucks and a tiny set of wheels. They headed out to the nearest parking lot to learn heelflips, kickflips and 360 flips, knowing that their survival as bona fide skaters depended on it.

The younger skaters started buying up videos by the dozen, since it was through the videos that they were going to learn all the new tricks, the hot skater of the moment and what you needed to be wearing to session your local spot. Ever since the Bones Brigade's first film, videos had played a part in the direction skateboarding took, but now they had eclipsed contests as the indicator of where skateboarding was heading.

The following year, Plan B released their second video, *Virtual Reality*. A breakout part by Sean

Sheffey showed how you could pull off technical street-skating lines with style to boot. Sheffey could float huge ollies *and* pull the most technical flip tricks going. The best part was, he made it look easy. Kids everywhere began concentrating on keeping their style loose, just like Sheffey.

For his part, Mullen once again outdid himself, blasting darkslides (sliding on the flipside of his board) across ledges and flipping his board back and forth in ways people had never imagined. Rodney may have dominated freestyle skateboarding back in the 1980s, but his two first Plan B parts showed the kids he was far from done. Even now, over 12 years later, he's still breaking out new tricks for every video part he puts together.

Plan B went on to release two more videos, but by then the rest of the skateboarding world had caught up, and Mike Ternasky's company wasn't the only one to watch. The Plan B team eventually split up after an internal dispute, and skater Rick Howard, who had been with the company since the beginning, formed Girl Skateboards, one of the most influential and long-lasting teams in skating. Howard poached some of the best riders from Plan B to flesh out his team, including Mike Carroll. Plan B still had Colin and Danny, and Mike Ternasky was determined to make a go of it. Shortly after, though, tragedy struck. The founding father of the team that set the course for modern street skating died in a car accident in 1994. With no one at the helm, Plan B finally folded, and its team members were forced to find new sponsors.

Twelve years later, Danny, Colin, Pat and the crew are back. Plan B relaunched itself in 2004 with one of the heaviest teams imaginable. They've added young guns Darrell Stanton, PJ Ladd, Ryan Gallant and Paul Rodriguez to their roster, and they're already making waves in the skateboarding community. Whether Plan B Version 2.0 will have the same effect on the skateboarding landscape as Version 1.0 is debatable, but with the team they've assembled, there's no doubt they have a head start.

Chapter Sixteen

Sponsor Me

The word "professional" is taken for granted. It's totally different today. There used to be only like, 10 guys—you could count how many pros there were on two hands. It's different now.

–Rick Howard, Transworld Skateboarding.
September 1996

When the street craze hit hard in the early 1990s, skateboarding exploded onto the scene once again. Skaters were dictating style everywhere, not just among themselves. All the way from their sneakers to their hooded sweat-tops and baseball hats, skaters were defining the outsider look, the underdog, the anti-jock. So many people tried to profit from the sport/subculture's growing popularity that skateboard companies were suddenly a dime-a-dozen. Using logos and graphics ripped from the most recognizable brands—Coca-Cola, Chiquita Bananas, Calvin

Klein—these companies screamed irreverence, and kids listened.

Most of the new skateboard companies began releasing videos, as well, realizing that it was the best way to showcase the talents of their riders and drum up support for their products. "Between contests, magazines, going on tour, the kids seeing you in person and videos, videos are probably the biggest part of it," said Rick Howard during an interview for his pro spotlight in *Transworld Skateboarding* in 1996.

"For professional skateboarding, the video is king. It's the demo, contest win and feature interview all rolled into one blazing package. If you've got something to prove, the VHS tape is your audition and the skaters of the world your audience. A sick video can turn a hometown hero into a household name and a middling pro into a legend," Michael Burnett wrote in *Thrasher* in 2003.

By showing skaters pulling trick after trick, with most of the falls and failed attempts edited out, videos raised the bar in a big way. Kids everywhere were suddenly aware of what could be done on a skateboard if they really put their minds to it. They bought the videos, went to the demos and contests and tried their damnedest to learn all the hot, new street tricks. Then they sent their own demo tapes to every company they could think of, in hopes of securing some sort of deal with the company for free merchandise. This way, they could brag to their friends that they were "sponsored," a badge of honour among skaters akin to being knighted in medieval Europe.

"Tricks had always been promoted via word of mouth," wrote Joey Tershay in Independent's history of skateboarding, *Built to Grind*. "But magazines couldn't keep up with all the new moves. Videos were more convenient, and "sponsor me" tapes became young hopefuls' preferred method of hooking themselves up. Every suburban kid must have had a tape."

One young skater who made a tape was Andrew Reynolds from Florida. But as Andrew admits in a *Thrasher* interview, he never even got around to sending it to anyone because he was too busy skating. Not a bad strategy, as it turned out. Soon after getting noticed at a contest in Florida, Andrew was filming for his own short part in the Birdhouse video *Ravers*. He was the rare exception, a kid with enough raw talent to barge right into the skateboarding world without sending off even one sponsor-me video.

"The first time I ever met Andrew, he was just this tiny, rail-thin, gaunt kid who could just flip his board anytime, and it was like the board was bigger than him, almost," said Tony Hawk in *Thrasher*'s *Skater of the Year* video. "Yeah, we were just like, 'We really want to sponsor you.'"

The immensely talented youngster ended up being in the right place at the right time, too, which meant he didn't have to rely on his tape. For another talented young skater named Jamie Thomas, who hailed from Alabama of all places, it took a bit more work and a whole lot of sponsor-me tapes to get noticed.

"Jamie Thomas has talent, but let's face it—talent is not enough. In the face of adversity, Jamie continues to conquer. Jamie is the visionary with the desire and ambition to see it through, every step of the way. He's an ever-scrapping, ever-hungry, 100-percent American mutt," wrote Greg Ware in *Thrasher* in August, 2004.

Long before Ware wrote those words, Jamie was a skater kid just like any other, obsessed with the idea of becoming a professional skateboarder. But unlike most of his peers, when it came to getting sponsored, Jamie refused to take no for an answer.

In 1984, a young Jamie Thomas found an old fibreglass skateboard in the attic of his parent's home. He rode it around for about a year before buying his first board, a Sims with Bennett Trucks and OJ wheels.

Over the next few years, Jamie got heavily into skating. Seeing the *Bones Brigade Video Show* in 1987 stoked the fire within him. During the lean years of the Alabama skate scene in the late 1980s,

Jamie quit skating for a while to ride BMX, but by 1989 he was back at it, traveling to Pensacola, Florida, to compete in his first-ever skate contest. He was surprised and excited when he placed third.

Jamie was heavily influenced by the street skating he saw in videos put out by the H-Street skateboard company in the late 1980s.

"I liked Hensley's parts in the H-Street videos so much that I tried to skate and dress like him," Jamie said in an interview for *Thrasher*. He wasn't the only one. Every street skater at the time wanted to copy Matt Hensley's style.

By 1991, Jamie was getting noticed, thanks in part to his boundless energy and his drive to catch every trick he did on film. He sent hundreds of tapes to skate companies he wanted to sponsor him, eventually landing limited sponsorships from Thunder Trucks, Spitfire wheels and Real Skateboards.

Once he got his first positive responses from California, Jamie became obsessed with the idea of becoming a professional skater.

"I sent a video a month, seriously, for like a year and a half," he told *Skateboarder* in 1998. "I was the nightmare kid who'd never leave you alone. I would send a video, and I'd ask the mail lady how long it would take to get there, and she would say three days. On the third day I'd be calling up asking to see it they got it and what they thought of it."

Jamie was so bold, in fact, that he decided to send in a sponsor-me video of himself skateboarding naked. "When I got to California, everyone in skateboarding had seen it. I wasn't stoked. Whatever... I was just a kid and I didn't give a s**t. I was just going for it. I thought if maybe I sent them a video of me doing tricks naked, maybe that would at least get their attention to call me back."

In 1992, Jamie quit school to pursue his dream of becoming a professional skateboarder. He worked at Wendy's to save enough money to buy a car so he could drive to California. After living like a vagrant on the streets of San Francisco for more than three months, Jamie turned pro for a small skate company called Experience. He left the company soon afterwards and joined the Invisible skate team. During the summer of 1994, Jamie toured the States with Invisible, before quitting to join Ed Templeton's new company, Toy Machine.

Toy Machine released two videos in 1994, but it was their third video, *Welcome to Hell*, released in 1996, that would put the name Jamie Thomas on every skaters' lips. If the Plan B videos of the early 1990s set the standard of the time, *Welcome to Hell* raised the bar once again, mainly through Jamie's part. Jamie skated rails like nobody ever had before, leaping on any and every bar going down a set of stairs, seemingly without fear.

"Few have had a bigger influence on the modern skate video than Jamie Thomas," wrote Michael Burnett in *Thrasher* in 2003. "Starting with Toy Machine's *Welcome to Hell*, the groundbreaking skating got the treatment it deserved. JT sped up the action, tightened the filming and editing and put more than a bong-hit's worth of time into choosing the music—an all-killer, no-filler approach, the result of which was a freight train of a tape that made folks cover their eyes, scream out loud and most importantly, want to get out and skate."

Jamie's part was nothing short of gnarly, but the rest of the video was pretty amazing as well. The skateboarding world was particularly taken aback by the skateboarding of Elissa Steamer. Finally, a female to show all the other ladies out there that street skating wasn't just for the boys. Girls could also hurl themselves off steps, down rails and along ledges, alternately landing on their wheels or their elbows. Elissa did more tricks in her part than most male skateboarders could put together in a year. She also showed she could take a heavy slam or two when necessary, if that was the price she had to pay.

"Filming this video was the first time that I'd given a single project everything I had," Jamie told

Thrasher. "This part helped me discover my potential and understand the value of focus."

At around the same time the video was in production, Jamie decided to turn his fledgling clothing company, Zero, into a board company. The first Zero video, *Thrill Of It All*, came out, and it was another sledgehammer, further cementing the reputation of Jamie Thomas as street skateboarding's number one maniac.

During one scene, skater Aaron Harrison tries to ollie off the top of a tractor-trailer down into a very short, very steep asphalt bank. After bailing hard 14 times, Aaron makes the ollie. This is the kind of commitment Jamie looks for in his skaters. At the end of his own part, after assaulting some very long and high rails, some huge gaps and some serious ledges, Jamie jumps off what's still considered one of the highest gaps anyone has ever tried to land on a skateboard. Now known simply as the "Leap of Faith", the drop is almost two stories. In the shot, Jamie leaps over a railing into space. He grabs onto his board by the heel edge to steady it under his feet as he plummets toward the earth. He lands on his board, but the board literally explodes beneath his feet from the impact. It's gnarly to watch. Jamie walks away from the attempt without really hurting himself, but he doesn't return to try it again. Once is enough. When asked if he'll ever go back and try the Leap of Faith again, he's non-committal.

"It's not something I think about very often," he told *Thrasher* in 2003. "If I were done with everything I want to get, then I would probably think about it more often."

After *Thrill of it All*, Jamie told *Thrasher*, he needed to refocus and once again look inside himself to find the fire that had driven him to succeed at skating in the first place. "For the next two years I focused on learning new tricks and taking them as far as I possibly could."

Zero's movies that followed, *Misled Youth* (1999), *Dying to Live* (2002) and *New Blood* (2005), are equally insane and have kept Jamie Thomas and his crew at the top; not without a price, mind you. Over the years, Jamie has suffered at the hands of the rails he has dared to skate. He's torn the ACL in one of his knees twice, smashed his family jewels several times and suffered numerous concussions.

"There was a period of time where I hit my head a lot," he told *Thrasher*. "I don't know what was going on. I don't know if I was pushing it too hard, or if I didn't know what I was doing. But for about four or five years I hit my head two or three times a year where I was unconscious, drooling on the concrete."

On sacking himself, Jamie was equally candid.

"I've taken it to the nuts a few times," he said during his interview with *Thrasher*. "It's really sketchy 'cause you don't know if you're doing permanent damage. It's just one of those things; you're banging your nuts real hard and hoping for the best."

"I didn't know if I was even capable of having kids. ...Now, I'm thinking of putting some on ice in case I hit my nuts real hard and can't have any more kids."

Without a doubt, Jamie's willingness to put everything on the line for a video set the tone for the stuntman skating seen in most videos today. Unless you're a ridiculously smooth, unbelievably technical street skater like Ronnie Creager, Daewon Song or PJ Ladd, you had better be willing to put yourself through some pain trying to drop big hammer tricks, or there's no place for you at the top echelons of the sport.

Every top pro nowadays is capable of putting together parts with very technical lines, very burly tricks or both at the same time, as in the case of Finland's Arto Saari, France's Bastien Salabanzi, Toronto's Mark Appleyard or Vancouver's Rick McCrank. Attacking rails with the daredevil-like commitment of Jamie Thomas and the technical prowess of Rodney Mullen is the standard set by skaters like Heath Kirchart, Geoff Rowley, Andrew Reynolds and, more recently, Billy Marks, Leo Romero and Kevin Long. There are so many skaters out there pushing technical street skating to new heights, that it would take many more pages to list them all. Chances are there are half a dozen down at your local skate spot who could give anyone circa 1995 a run for their money.

Every year, more and more nobodies come out of the woodwork ready to blow minds. Even young kids like Ryan Sheckler, who was winning pro contests by the time he was 12 years old, and Nyjah Houston, a top-ranked amateur at the age of 11, are capable of upping the ante on huge rails and drops, to say nothing of what they could show you at your local skatepark. Trying to categorize skaters as either vert, pool, ramp, technical street or burly gap skaters is pointless nowadays. Just as soon as you've got your mind made up that such-and-such skater is a handrail skater, he or she'll drop into the local pool and launch into the biggest frontside stalefish grab (where you grab the heel edge of your board between your feet with your back hand) that you have ever seen.

With millions of kids skating, new skateparks cropping up every day, and legions of innovators pushing the sport to new heights year after year, it's finally beginning to look like skateboarding is here to stay. The death of skateboarding seems as likely now as the death of any major league sport in North America.

Chapter Seventeen

The X-Games: Skateboarding Meets Popular Culture

In 1994, competitive skateboarding got a boost with the launch of World Cup Skateboarding (WCS), an organizing body that replaced the National Skateboarding Association.

The WCS held its first event, called Slam City Jam, in May 1994 in Vancouver. The following year, the WCS came up with a ranking system for street and vert. Ed Templeton was crowned the first World Champion of street, and Mike Frazier took top honors in vert.

That same year, ESPN contacted the WCS to see about organizing skateboarding competitions in their new X-Games. As Tony Hawk recalls in his autobiography, *Occupation: Skateboarder*, everyone in the skateboarding world, including Tony himself, was confused about what to do when it came to the X-Games, a hugely corporate event that threatened to suck the soul right out of skateboarding. "My curiosity got the best of me, and since they were having a vert event (which were few and far between), I decided to go," he wrote.

Good thing for Tony, whose career and popularity received a much-needed boost when he finished first in the vert contest and second in street at the first-ever X-Games in June 1995.

"The contest aired a week later, and the amount of exposure it generated was amazing," he wrote. "People began to recognize me on the street, in the mall and in video stores. I'd been recognized before, but it had always been by skateboarders; now civilians came up to tell me they'd seen me on television."

Tony had managed to stay in the skateboarding game after leaving Powell and starting up his own company, Birdhouse, with fellow former Bones Brigader Per Welinder. After Tony's win at the X-Games, he won several more big vert contests, and his company became one of the most popular in skateboarding. But Tony knew, as any skater in the 1990s did, that you couldn't just stay relevant to other skaters by winning contests. You had to release a good video, as well.

Birdhouse released a groundbreaking video in 1998, *The End*, which showcased the incredible street skating of up-and-comers Andrew Reynolds and Rick McCrank, the clean style and technical ability of street skater Willy Santos and amazing parts by Steve Berra and Bucky Lasek. The standout part, though, features established street superstars Heath Kirchart and Jeremy Klein skating at night wearing black Armani suits, using lights to illuminate the giant street obstacles they were ollieing on (including a bus shelter!) with the help of a bright green jump ramp. The part, edited to David Bowie's *Under Pressure,* also features a van exploding and a dream sequence in which hired actresses dressed as sexy maids set up Heath and Jeremy's boards as the boys busy themselves playing video games in a giant mansion. It finishes with Heath and Jeremy on fire skating down a pier and jumping off a ramp into the ocean.

The movie ends with Tony skating a giant vert ramp Tim Payne built for him in a bullfighting ring in Mexico. Beside the ramp, Payne constructed a giant wooden loop. Nobody had really tried the loop since Duane Peters apparently made it all the way around in the 1970s. No photographic evidence exists of Peters' make, but it's accepted as fact among skaters that it happened. After some practice and at least one heavy fall, Tony skated down the giant in-ramp, shot into the loop, went upside down and exited the other side. It was done. There was only one other trick on Tony's wish list that he wanted to include in the film, the elusive 900 (airing out of the vert ramp and spinning two-and-a-half revolutions in the air before re-entering). Unfortunately, despite several bold attempts, it wasn't going to happen.

Nursing a sore back, Tony was forced to shelve the trick for another day.

The End was definitely over the top. Filmed entirely on 16-mm and 35-mm film stock by acclaimed action film director Jamie Mosberg, *The End* had more production values than all the skateboarding movies that came before it combined. It was a big-budget affair, but the impression it left in the saturated video marketplace made the expense worthwhile. The movie was a huge hit. It wasn't going to appear in cinemas alongside the next *Star Wars* entry any time soon, but skaters appreciated the effort, and it once again raised the bar for skateboarding videos.

The Birdhouse film, in spite of its name, didn't really spell the end for Tony. He still had to land the 900 before he could call it quits, if not from skateboarding entirely, at least from competitive skating. By the time the movie came out, he was burnt out on competing and decided he would call it quits after the last contest of the year. The 900 haunted him, but he never thought his battle with the elusive maneuver would end the way it did at the fifth X-games in San Francisco in 1999.

As Tony explains in his book, the 900 was proving difficult for all of the world's top vert skaters to land, simply because after trying the trick a few times you were usually so beat up you didn't want to try it again for a long while.

"After 10 or so attempts, you felt as if you'd just walked away from a car crash," he explains.

In spite of almost landing the trick in 1996, the 900 continued to elude Tony—until that evening at the X-Games. Tony placed third in the vert event earlier that day. His teammate Bucky Lasek won. As Tony recalls in his book, he was happy for his friend, but, ever the competitor, he was hardly happy about placing third in what would be his last appearance in a vert contest at the X-Games (though he would continue to dominate the vert doubles contest with Andy Macdonald for years to come).

A huge crowd had gathered by the time the vert "Best Trick" contest had started. Skaters Bob Burnquist, Bucky Lasek and Colin McKay were all in contention, armed with difficult tricks that nobody else could pull. For his first shot at the prize money, Tony pulled a varial 720 (two full rotations while grabbing the board and spinning it an extra 180 degrees), but he wasn't sure the trick was enough to win. He decided to try spinning a 900. "I wasn't that serious. I just thought I'd crank a few," he wrote of his decision to try the trick.

But he was coming close. The stunt that had eluded him for so many years suddenly seemed doable. The crowd screamed for more action. Tony delivered, trying the dangerous trick over and over again. On his 12th try, he spun the 900 and landed smoothly on the transition of the ramp. He'd finally pulled it! He squatted from the impact and dragged his hand slightly on the landing, but the 900 was conquered. Everyone in attendance, realizing the significance of what they had just witnessed, went nuts, running onto the ramp to congratulate the skateboarding legend who had just made history.

Chapter Eighteen

Global Skateboarding Madness

By the time Tony Hawk landed the 900 at the X-Games in 1999, skateboarding had long since achieved global domination. As the sport gained in popularity, more and more skaters started appearing at contests from countries all over the world.

Nobody knew who Brazil's Rodil de Araujo Jr. was when he showed up in North America and began dominating street contests, winning gold at the 1996 and 1998 X-Games. Meanwhile, Canadians like Rick McCrank, Mark Appleyard, Paul Machnau, Max Dufour and Pierre-Luc Gagnon were following in the footsteps of fellow countryman Colin McKay, showing the skateboard world that it wasn't all about snowmobiles and hockey north of the border. Today, one of the main riders on Rodney Mullen's new team is Vancouver native Chris Haslam, one of the most technically proficient street skaters ever.

Hot-shot Geoff Rowley from Liverpool, England, and fellow countryman Tom Penny had been holding down in the streets of California for years by the time Arto Saari showed up from Finland, and the skateboarding world first witnessed the amazing skills of French teenager Bastien Salabanzi.

Australia, with its warm, dry climate, is a natural fit for skateboarding, and the country consistently churns out top-level skaters, including vert brothers Tas and Ben Pappas, rail rider Matt Mumford and vert-rager-turned-extreme-TV-host Jason Ellis. Most recently, the daredevil antics and don't-give-a-damn attitude of Aussie street destroyer Dustin Dollin have earned him a top spot among the select group of every teenage boy's favorite skateboarders.

When it comes to top skaters from outside the U.S., though, most discussions start and end with the name Bob Burnquist. Growing up on the mean streets of Rio de Janeiro, sniffing glue and skateboarding, Bob one day found himself confronted with a choice: pursue skating or keep hanging out with his friends and getting high. Thankfully for the skateboarding world, he chose to keep riding. Bob struggled with drinking, drugs and partying for a while longer before giving up all the bad stuff entirely after almost destroying his knee during a hangover session.

In 1995, the Brazilian showed up at Slam City Jam in Vancouver and put all the other vert skaters to shame. From that day on, he continued to dominate vert contests, earning numerous top three spots and garnering *Thrasher*'s coveted Skater of the Year award in 1997.

Bob's specialty is skating switch-stance, in other words, being able to do his tricks while rolling backward. Skating switch adds an element of difficulty only someone who's ever tried to roll down a hill backward on a skateboard can appreciate.

In 2001, the organizers of the annual Tampa Pro skateboard contest in Tampa, Florida, set up a loop outside the skatepark and challenged all comers to give it a shot. It had been several years since Tony Hawk had filmed the loop for his film, *The End,* and every skater knew it was possible. The question was, if Tony wasn't there, who else was going to step up and give it a try? As it turned out, there were plenty of people willing to stick their necks out. Before long, Al Partenan, Peter Hewitt and Bob had all stepped up and nailed the loop. The crowd went berserk every time, but little did they know, Bob was about to try something that, if he made it, would cement his place in the skateboarding history books—the switch loop.

When Bob started trying the loop switch, Peter Hewitt stepped to it again, this time bailing and sending himself to the hospital. Falling from the top of a 10-foot-high loop is no joke. People could hardly believe what they were seeing. The carnage was unprecedented; the gnar-factor had seen no equal. Soon after Peter's fall, another skater, Brian Schaffer, flipped onto his head during a loop attempt and followed Peter in another ambulance to the hospital. After that, the crowd thinned dramatically. Two ambulances? The show had to be over. Not so. Bob climbed back up to the top of the entry ramp, dropped in switch and nailed the loop. The crowd went absolutely ballistic. It was the most insane thing any of them had ever seen, or are likely to ever see.

The next year, Bob stormed onto the upside-down skateboarding scene once again; this time he tried to complete a full loop of the infamous Mount Baldy Pipeline. A loop constructed specifically for the purpose of going upside down on a skateboard has a long ramp going down into it that the skater uses to gather speed to get all the way around. It also has an exit ramp, meaning the skater isn't forced to deal with another transition right after completing a full-speed loop. None of this exists at Mount Baldy. All that's there is a massive, rough concrete full pipe about 14 feet high. Just carving high up on its walls is a gnarly feat worthy of any skateboarding magazine cover. Trying to loop the thing is unheard of.

When Bob went for it, everyone in attendance realized that he was literally putting his life on the line. If he bailed from the top down onto his head, he would die. No question. What happened next? Bob bailed. Luckily, he was somehow able to pull off a backflip mid-fall and land on his feet. The effect of the fall on everybody watching was intense, as Keith David Hamm describes in his book, *Scarred for Life*.

"Lance (Mountain) nearly had a heart attack. Salba 'bout s**t his shorts. The others shook their heads and stared and blinked and gulped with what could be described only as utter disbelief."

Bob wasn't phased. He was too focused on the task at hand to worry about a fall. He walked back to his starting point and began carving the wall to try it again.

Bob tried to loop Baldy 14 times, crashing heavily on several attempts. He almost made it, but on his last try, he landed funny and broke his foot.

The next year, Bob tried his unprecedented stunt on another full-pipe, a 12-foot-high steel pipe used as a prop in a skateboard commercial featuring his wife, skateboarder Jen O'Brien. This time, he made no mistakes, riding high up on the wall before powering a carve right upside down and cruising the full way around the pipe. Watching the clip is a strange experience. It doesn't seem possible that someone could have done what Bob did.

Chapter Nineteen

Danny Way: Skateboarding's Next Frontier

Just when it started to look like nothing new could be done in skateboarding, Danny Way came along and started building massive ramps that would blast him higher into the air than any other skateboarder had ever gone before.

It all started in 1997, when Danny's shoe company, DC Shoes, built the super ramp, a giant halfpipe designed to help him shatter the world record for the highest air on a skateboard. It worked. Danny blew the record away, soaring more than 16 feet above the half-pipe. As if that wasn't enough action for one day, Danny then decided to jump out of a helicopter into the giant ramp. The stunt, dubbed the bomb drop, together with the new world record, earned Danny the cover of *Transworld Skateboarding* and a ton of coverage in other skateboard magazines. While some photographers were invited to take pictures at the DC ramp event, others, knowing the event would be huge and couldn't be missed, shot Danny from outside the compound.

Over the next few years, things slowed down somewhat for Danny after he suffered numerous injuries. Between 1999 and 2002, Danny underwent seven surgeries, five on his knee and two on his shoulder. Several years before that, in 1994, Danny broke his neck in a freak surfing accident. No stranger to pain, as soon as Danny recovered from his injuries, he got back on his board and began pushing the limits again.

In 2002, Danny built the first "Mega Ramp," a giant ramp shaped like a snowboard jump. It had a huge roll-in and a long gap between the take-off ramp and the landing ramp. Riding the Mega Ramp, Danny shattered the distance record for a jump on a skateboard, soaring 65 feet over the gap and landing smoothly on the other side. Further down from the Mega Ramp, Danny had constructed a massive quarter-pipe wall. With the speed he generated from the long-distance jump, he was able to launch himself over 18 feet out of the top of the quarter-pipe, splintering his old highest-air record. The new record wouldn't stand for long. Danny, not satisfied to go down in the history books only once, built a larger set-up the next year and blew away both his distance jump record and his height record.

Danny also began pulling tricks over the Mega Ramp gap, and not just any tricks either: frontside 360s, 540s, then frontside 360 heelflips (spinning a 360 while flipping his board with his heel before grabbing it). When *The DC Video* came out in 2003, it was the biggest thing to hit the skateboarding world in a long time. The other DC skaters all had amazing parts too, but Danny's part at the end of the video blew everyone away.

"I can't emphasize enough how innovative and difficult his entire video part was," veteran skater Chris Miller told *The Skateboard Mag* for the article on Danny that appeared in their premier issue.

After *The DC Video* came out, Danny went back to the ramp and hauled a giant wooden box topped with a giant rail up onto the top of the landing ramp. He laid down street-oriented tricks on the rail, such as heelflip railslides (flipping his board before landing in a boardslide on the monster rail), 270 slides (spinning himself three quarters of the way around before landing in a board slide on the rail) and even a switch nose grind (ollieing off the take-off backward and landing on the rail with his front truck for a grind). All this after launching off the take-off ramp and over the huge gap.

The footage of the box and rail tricks made it onto the deluxe edition of *The DC Video* DVD. Skaters couldn't believe their eyes. Most of the tricks Danny did were difficult enough to imagine trying to do on a small railing down a few stairs. Hardly anyone could conceive of trying them on a massive rail shaped like a banana after flying off a giant ramp and over a huge gap. It was psychotic.

Danny Way's career reads like a history of modern skateboarding. Unlike Bob Burnquist, who came out of nowhere to climb atop the heap of professional vert skaters in the late 1990s, Danny was there every step of the way. He's haunted the professional skateboard scene ever since he was a little grommet (a skater term for a little kid eager to impress the older guys).

Danny can't remember when he got his first skateboard, but he remembers pushing around the Del Mar skatepark as a six-year-old. He was constantly trying to make an impression on his older brother, Damon, and Damon's friend. "I thought if I did tricks that maybe those guys couldn't throw down, they'd think I was somewhat cool. That was my main motivation to skateboard," he told *Transworld Skateboarding* in an interview in September 2002.

Before too long, Danny was flying over backyard ramps, doing tricks even Damon wasn't willing to try. Things moved pretty fast once Danny focused his seemingly limitless energy on becoming the best skateboarder around. He entered his first vert contest, at Del Mar, before he turned 13. Soon after that, he got his own ramp and learned tricks like bonelesses, backside airs and even McTwists. Sponsorship was inevitable.

Hanging out at Del Mar every day, Danny met and befriended Mark "Gator" Rogowski, who offered to help him get on a limited sponsorship with Vision. "Anything for free at the time was amazing, so I jumped right on that program with Gator and rode for Vision for a while."

In 1988, Danny quit Vision to join the Bones Brigade, the team he had wanted to be a part of ever since he started skating. But after six months, Danny quit Powell when they refused to send him to a contest he wanted to attend in Houston. Danny called Mike Ternasky, who was running H-Street at the time with ex-pro skater Tony Magnusson, and they agreed to send Danny if he would come and ride for their team. Danny credits Mike with guiding him through the difficult stage of his life when he had to adjust to becoming a top professional skateboarder traveling the world.

"He became a huge role model for me," Danny told *Transworld*. "Mike was a guy who had already been there, done that with a lot of things and was really smart. On top of that, not only was he wise, but he had good common sense knowledge to drop down on me. When you're 14, not in school, traveling around the world, hanging out with guys like Gator and Hosoi and the skateboard legends and partying like crazy—you need guidance."

Danny's need for guidance was only strengthened by the fact that he grew up in a broken home.

His mother divorced his stepfather when Danny was just a little kid, then his mother got into drugs and started dating lowlifes who would beat her in front of Danny and his brother. The domestic chaos was constant throughout Danny's early days as a pro skateboarder. "The only thing that really pulled me out of it was skateboarding," he told *Transworld*. "It got me to the point where I could step back, look at it and go, 'You guys can have it. I'm outta here.'"

Eventually, Danny grew tired of being on the H-Street team. It became too diluted for his liking. Mike was signing on too many riders, and Danny wanted to be on a tighter team where he knew everyone. So, when Mark Gonzales and Jason Lee asked him if he wanted to join them on Blind, he jumped at the chance.

Blind was the best thing going at the time, and Danny loved being on the team. But after two years, Mike Ternasky began talking with Danny about starting a new team. The idea grew, and then Mike started Plan B. The team attracted a lot of the best skaters at the time, including Danny and Canadian Colin McKay.

"I was about to ride for Blind Skateboards," Colin told *Transworld*. "Rick Howard was like, 'Hey, you should ride for Plan B.' Danny was my idol, and Plan B was with Blind at World Industries, so it didn't matter to me who I rode for. Blind was the f*****g coolest thing at the time, right next to

Plan B. They were always neck and neck. I can remember the exact moment when I was like, 'Hey, I'm on Plan B'."

Both Danny and Colin stayed with Plan B until its demise, becoming famous for their ability to ride anything. Danny and Colin's ability to take street-inspired tricks onto vert ramps and vice-versa breathed new life into skateboarding at a time when a little fresh air was what the sport needed to stay alive.

"I've found from all the years I spent skating street that it's taught me to skate vert a whole different way," Danny would say many years later.

In 1994, disaster struck when Danny broke his neck surfing. Unsure whether he would ever skate again, he embarked on an aggressive year-long rehabilitation program. He returned to competitive skateboarding at the Tampa Pro vert contest in Florida in 1995. Still in pain from the injury, he claimed first place.

Two years later, Danny decided to build the giant half-pipe known as the DC Super Ramp and try to break the world record for the highest air on a skateboard. Ever since then, Danny has dominated the airways with his big ramp skating. Nobody can ever touch what he did for the sport when he started building his super structures and launching himself higher and farther than anyone had ever thought possible on a skateboard.

In the summer of 2005, there was a big air skateboarding competition in the X-Games, and other skateboarders like Pierre-Luc Gagnon, Bob Burnquist and Bucky Lasek threw themselves off the giant-sized ramps in hopes of winning gold, but, of course, Danny won it—in spite of a massively sprained ankle.

Earlier that same summer, as if all the things he'd accomplished in skateboarding over the previous few years weren't enough, Danny decided to go to China, build the biggest damn skateboarding ramp anyone had ever built and launch himself over the Great Wall of China. On his first attempt, he barely made it over the wall, landing hard on his feet on the flat deck at the top of the landing ramp and wrecking his ankle.

Everyone thought Danny's battle with the Wall was over. It wasn't. The next day, Danny taped up his ankle, injected it with all sorts of drugs, went right back up to the giant roll-in ramp, dropped in and launched over the wall. He was sure to make it over this time. With so much time in the air, Danny considered putting his board under his feet, but decided against it. Instead, he slid out on his kneepads. He had made it over the distance, though, and in his mind, the jump was already a done deal.

On his third attempt, Danny rocketed down the take-off at over 50 miles per hour, confident he was going to make it over. In the air, he grabbed his board and held on, landing cleanly on the landing ramp on the other side, before shooting along the flat bottom below the landing ramp and up off the biggest quarter-pipe ever built into a 25-foot high backside air. "His board goes varial, but he still manages to catch it Indy, again thinks about putting it back, and again smartly decides against it, free-falling nearly 45 feet from the sky onto his knees and into the tranny," recalled Danny's friend and former pro vert skater Jason Ellis in an article he wrote about the event for *Transworld*.

After the make, Danny went back up and launched a 360 over the gap, which is sort of like laughing in the face of someone holding a gun to your head and then maybe spitting on their shoe.

Sticking with the theme during a press conference afterward, Danny told the assembled members of the media, "It's a war out there, and when you're in a war, people shoot at ya, and when people shoot at ya, you gotta shoot back, and I won the battle." Knowing Danny, there'll be plenty more battles to come. As can be said for every skater out there, there's always another trick out there you've gotta land.

Notes on Sources

ARTICLES

Alva, Tony. "Dog Tails." *Thrasher.* October 1995.

Beato, G. "The Lords of Dogtown." *Spin.* March 1999.

Bolster, Warren. "Henry Hester." *Skateboarder,* Vol 3., No. 6. July 1977.

Burnett, Michael. "Lance Mountain Interview." *Thrasher,* June 2002.

Burnett, Michael. "Countdown: Dying to Live" *Thrasher.* Jan. 2003.

Cliver, Sean. "The 15 Most Coveted Skateboards Ever." *Transworld Skateboarding.* April 2005.

Donelly, Joe. "The Ghosts of Dogtown." *The LA Weekly.* August, 2001.

Ellis, Jason. "The Massive Attack." *Transworld Skateboarding.* November 2005.

Gillogly, Brian. "Who's Hot! Kim Cespedes. " *Skateboarder.* Vol 3, No. 3. Feb. 1977.

Gillogly, Brian. "Who's Hot! Ellen Oneal." *Skateboarder.* Vol. 3, No. 3.Feb. 1977.

Goodrich, Jim. "Steve Cathey." *Skateboarder.* Vol. 5, No. 2. September 1978.

Hesselgrave, Curtis. "Who's Hot! Tom Inouye." *Skateboarder.* Vol. 3, No. 5. June 1977.

J-Soy. "25 Years to Life: Steve Caballero." *Concrete Powder.* Issue 79. November 2005.

Johnson, Cory "Free Fallin': how Skateboard King Mark "Gator" Anthony was Born Again as a Rapist & a Murderer" *The Village Voice.* December 8, 1992.

Laine, Phil. "Who's Hot! Shogo Kubo." *Skateboarder.* Vol. 4, No. 5. Dec. 1977.

Marcus, Ben. "Interview with Stacy Peralta." Surfer. 2004.

Miles "Savannah Slamma 3." *Thrasher.* Sept. 1989.

Olson, Steve. "Lance Mountain Interview. *Juice*. Issue 54.

Phelps, Jake. "Product Patrol" *Thrasher*. August 1990.

Phelps, Jake. "The Legend of Danny Way." *Thrasher*. Sept. 2003.

Phelps, Jake. "*Thrasher*: Twenty Five Years." *Thrasher*. Jan. 2006.

Rogowski, Mark "Why I Did It." *Thrasher*. April 1996.

Smythe, Jon. "Tony Alva." *Skateboarder*. Vol. 3, No. 3. February 1977.

Smythe, Jon. "Tony Alva. Second Interview." *Skateboarder*. Vol.4, No.11. July 1978.

Smythe, Jon. "Stacy Peralta Interview." *Skateboarder*. Volume 3, # 1. October 1976.

Stecyk, C. R. "Aspects of the downhill Slide." *Skateboarder*. Vol. 2, No. 2. Fall 1975.

Stricker, Eric. "Paycheck: Christian Hosoi." *Transworld Skateboarding*. Volume 23 Issue 1. Feb. 2005.

Thatcher, Kevin. "Savannah Slamma." *Thrasher*. Dec. 1987.

Thatcher, Kevin. "Grab that Board." *Thrasher*. January 1981.

Ware, Greg. "Ten years of Thomas: What Constitutes a Great Skateboard Career?" *Thrasher*. August 2004.

Wilkins, Kevin. "Danny Way: Pro Spotlight." *Transworld Skateboarding*. Sept. 2002.

Wilkins, Kevin. "Rick Howard: Pro Spotlight." *Transworld Skateboarding*. Sept. 1996.

Wilkins, Kevin. "Back in the Day." *Transworld Skateboarding*. May 2005.

Wilkins, Kevin. "Danny Way: Unfinished Business." *The Skateboard Mag*. April 2004.

Wilkins, Kevin. "Fahrenheit 540 (degrees): 20 years of the Twist". *Thrasher*, Sept. 2004.

Wilkins, Kevin. "Pool Riding Symposium." *Skateboarder*. Vol. 3, No. 1. October 1976.

WEB

http://salbaland.com/music.html.

Peralta, Stacy. Article by Stacy Peralta, 1999. http://www.ollieair.com/

Pearson, Jesse. "Never Mind the Dogtown: Stoked Skates and Destroys."

http://www.viceland.com/issues/v9n8/htdocs/never.php

Skateboard Museum. http://www.skullskates.com/museum/intro.html.

www.dannyway.com

www.oldschoolskateboarding.com

www.skateboardermag.com

www.skateboarding.com

www.thrashermagazine.com

  http://www.thrashermagazine.com/index.php?SCREEN=interview_cab

  http://secure.thrashermagazine.com/index.php?SCREEN=interviews_jamiethomas&page_num=1

Jamie Thomas: Web Exclusive.

Steve Caballero: Web Exclusive.

Z-boys. Official site. http://www.angelfire.com/ca2/dtown/

  Adams, Jay. Z-boys Interview. http://www.angelfire.com/ca2/jayadams/2001.html

  Wentzle Ruml III Interview. http://www.angelfire.com/ca2/dtown/ruml2001.html

FILMS

CBC television report. "Skurfing the Streets in '65". *Across Canada*. June 15, 1965.

Dogtown and Z-Boys. Stacy Peralta. 2001.

Hokus-Pokus. H-Street. 1989

Questionable. Plan B. 1992.
Shackle Me Not. H-Street. 1988
Stoked: the Rise and Fall of Gator. Helen Stickler. 2003.
Street on Fire, Santa Cruz. 1989.
The DC Video. DC Shoes. 2003.
The End. Birdhouse. 1998.
The Search For Animal Chin. Powell & Peralta. 1986.
Thrill of it All. Zero, 1997.
Video Days. Blind. 1991.
Virtual Reality. Plan B. 1993.
Welcome to Hell. Toy Machine. 1996.
Wheels of Fire. Santa Cruz. 1988

BOOKS

Brooke, Michael. *The Concrete Wave: The History of Skateboarding*. Toronto: Warwick Publishing, 1999.

Denike Bob (Editor). *Built To Grind*. San Francisco: High Speed Productions, 2004.

Friedman, Glen E. and C.R. Stecyk III. *Dogtown, The Legend of the Z-Boys*. New York: Burning Flags Press, 2000.

Hamm, Keith David. *Scarred for Life*. San Francisco: Chronicle Books LLC, 2004.

Hawk, Tony (with Sean Mortimer). *Hawk: Occupation Skateboarder*. New York: Regan Books. 2001.

Mullen, Rodney and Sean Mortimer. *The Mutt: How to Skateboard and Not Kill Yourself*. New York: HarperCollins, 2004.

Weyland, Jocko. *The Answer is Never*. New York: Grove Press, 2002.

Tom Peacock

Tom Peacock is a freelance journalist and writer living in Montreal, Québec. He got his start in writing at *The Ubyssey*, the University of British Columbia's student newspaper. He's since worked for the *Sherbrooke Record*, and as a contributing editor and writer for *Verge* magazine. He's also the author of *Snowboarding: Extreme Stories from Canada's Best Riders*.

When Tom's not trying to finish an article, he can be found at the offices of *Our Canada* magazine, where he works as a contributing editor, or down at the local skatepark trying over and over again to land a trick he swears he once landed—"Just one more try, then we can go."